The
Somatic
Yoga
Toolbox

Isabelle Mullesch

1

TABLE OF CONTENTS

2

INTRODUCTION:

WHO IS THE BOOK FOR?

This book is aimed at the stressed/anxious and those who get angry a little quickly, the melancholic and the overexcited, ultimately everyone. It's obviously designed for those who struggle with an overactive nervous system, those who are stuck in the fight or flight mode.

The exercises are intended to be easy to do and remember and can be practiced on your own or with family.

They are based on knowledge of polyvagal theory and that of the nervous system, and inspired by the traditions of Tai Chi and Yoga. They are also based on the notions of acceptance as developed in ACT therapy, one of the most effective cognitive-behavioral therapies for improving quality of life.

This book will help you to learn how to manage your emotions by going through the body and learning techniques that will allow you to manage your emotions and your stress on a daily basis, techniques that are easy to learn and can be used by everyone, without the need for be particularly physically fit or flexible. It's an holistic way to reboot communication brain to body.

To be practiced alone or with others and without moderation for a calm nervous system in order to be well equipped to evolve with serenity in the modern world.

Go out of the fight or flight mode so you can start healing because when you are chronically ill, or just basically stressed or tired, the worst thing to have is a nervous system stuck in the fight or flight mode.

You want to be in the parasympathetic mode, so you can heal, rest and digest (food and what happens in your life)

But for that, the body needs to know it's safe.

That's the goal of this book.

Making your body safe so you can feel confortable in it, and live your life the best you can!

But I want to emphasize the fact that this is not a miracle cure, at all!

It's a practice and you will need to be consistent. It may provide some relief to a certain extent to some of your symptoms but I can't guarantee that.

The goal is to accept things as they currently are, so that your body stops fighting and that's where the healing and the magic begin.

WHO I AM?

A qualified yoga teacher for 12 years, diligent practitioner of yoga and meditation for 20 years, I am also trained in the TRE method (Tension and Trauma Releasing Exercises), somatic exercises and breathing techniques (Breathwork) such as cardiac coherence, as part of stress management.

But my main job is customer support manager, so I know what stress means ;-) !

I encounter, like many of us, medical difficulties in my life which led me to these practices, which help me a lot in my daily life as a single mother with several chronic illnesses (adrenal insufficiency and mast cell activation syndrome).

And as a mother, I also encounter challenges that somatic exercises help me to overcome or accept and which help my son to tame his emotions, which are often very intense ;-)

I have brought together these techniques in this book so that I can share them with as many people as possible.

I support you in creating your own toolbox so that you become completely autonomous in the management and acceptance of your emotions.

If you want personalized support in addition to this book, please note that my sessions consist of an exchange to understand your problem, then I offer you easy and easily reproducible exercises at home, physical exercises, breathing exercises, and changes to your lifestyle if this seems wise.

But you should be able to do this on your own with this book! At least, that's the goal ;-) !

Do not hesitate to contact me on isabelle.mullesch@gmail.com and see you soon to enjoy the magic of somatic exercises!

THE NERVOUS SYSTEM

We note that throughout time and in all cultures, vibrations, tremors and rocking have been used as therapeutic tools.

To understand the benefit of these practices, we must first understand how our nervous system works, at least in broad terms.

The central nervous system includes the brain, spinal cord and all the nerves in our body. The autonomic nervous system is the part of the central nervous system that regulates involuntary functions of the body. Within the autonomic nervous system are the sympathetic and parasympathetic nervous systems, both of which control the same body parts and general body functions, but with opposite effects.

Understanding what sympathetic and parasympathetic responses are is not essential for them to occur: they are involuntary responses to various stimuli. However, when we understand what each part of our autonomic nervous system does and what it needs to function properly, we become more effective at managing our stress.

THE SYMPATHETIC NERVOUS SYSTEM

The fight or flight response is well known, but what is perhaps less known is that this response to external stimuli relies entirely on the sympathetic nervous system. When we face a perceived threat of any kind, whether physical or emotional, our sympathetic nervous system kicks in and causes automatic, involuntary responses, such as increased heart rate, elevated blood pressure, increased awareness, increased respiratory rate and more sweating. The sympathetic nervous system also shuts down many parasympathetic responses in order to use more energy for the fight or flight response.

THE PARASYMPATHETIC NERVOUS SYSTEM

The parasympathetic nervous system affects the same bodily functions as the sympathetic nervous system, but in a completely different, or perhaps even opposite, way. It works by slowing down certain responses and bringing a state of calm to the body, allowing it to rest, relax and repair itself. The primary function of the parasympathetic nervous system is to maintain long-term health and a healthy balance in all functions of the body. Parasympathetic responses include increased digestive enzymes, decreased heart rate, constriction of the bronchi in the lungs, and more relaxed muscles.

WHY IT'S IMPORTANT?

The sympathetic and parasympathetic nervous systems are essential to our health and survival. However, for our bodies to live healthy and function properly for as long as possible, there must be a balance between the two. If there is a problem in communication between your brain and the impulses that promote sympathetic responses, your body will function in fight-or-flight mode too often and for far too long, which can have negative consequences for your overall health. We all know the effects of chronic stress on our body.

Spending so much time on alert is not only exhausting, but it can also be physically damaging. The physical consequences of acute stress can include high blood pressure, migraines and disorders such as fibromyalgia, chronic gastritis, burnout, depression, chronic anxiety, etc.

So we want a healthy balance between the two parts of your autonomic nervous system, and that happens when your spinal cord and nerves are functioning properly.

A PRECIOUS TOOL: THE VAGUS NERVE

WHAT IS THE VAGUS NERVE?

The vagus nerve, also known as the vagal nerves, is the main nerve in your parasympathetic nervous system. This system controls specific bodily functions such as your digestion, heart rate, and immune system. These functions are involuntary, meaning you cannot consciously control them.

Your left and right vagal nerves contain 75% of the nerve fibers in your parasympathetic nervous system. These fibers transmit information between your brain, heart, and digestive system.

The vagus nerves are the 10th of 12 cranial nerves. The vagus nerve is known as cranial nerve X, the Roman numeral meaning 10.

Your vagal nerves are part of your body's nervous system. They play an important role in involuntary sensory and motor functions, including:

- Digestion
- Heart rate, blood pressure and respiration
- Immune system responses
- Mood

14

- Heart rate, blood pressure and breathing
- Immune system responses
- Production of mucus and saliva
- Skin and muscle sensations
- Words
- Taste
- Urinary flow

Your vagus nerves are the longest cranial nerve, running from your brain to the large intestine. Your left vagus nerve runs down the left side of your body. The right vagus nerve runs down the right side of your body.

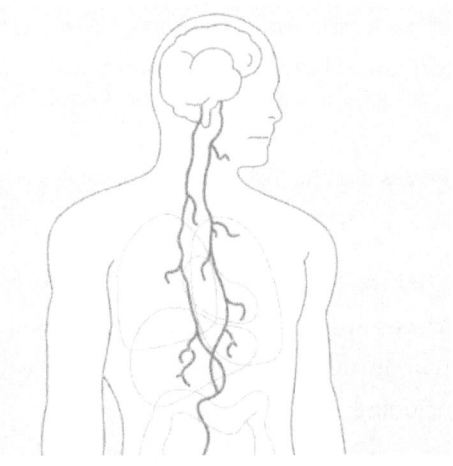

"Vagus" is the Latin word for wandering. Your vagal nerves run through your body in long, winding ways. They come out of your medulla oblongata in the lower part of the brainstem. Then the nerves pass through or connect to your:

- Neck (between the carotid artery and the jugular vein)
- Chest (thorax)
- Heart
- Lungs
- Abdomen and digestive tract

Specifically, the vagus nerve is part of the parasympathetic nervous system, which calms your body after a stressful situation. The vagus nerve transmits signals from your brain to other parts of your body, like your heart or intestines, to start this process.

Keeping your vagus nerve healthy involves doing many of the things you could do to stay healthy in general. Eat a balanced diet with plenty of fresh fruits and vegetables. Make sure you exercise for at least 30 minutes several times a week. Manage chronic health conditions like high blood pressure or diabetes. Additionally, practicing mindfulness, meditation can help keep your vagus nerve healthy by calming your nervous system.

Experts believe there is a strong connection between the gut microbiota and a healthy vagus nerve because the bacteria in our intestines can produce neurotransmitters such as dopamine and serotonin. So they suggest taking prebiotics and probiotics to keep your gut biome healthy.

Shaking, rocking, the purring of a cat, animals shaking themselves after stress, electroshock therapies, neurogenic tremors, chants and mantras that vibrate the vocal cords. A few examples that remind us that shaking is a powerful tool to bring calm to our body and mind because the vibrations stimulate certain parts of the vagus nerve.

Here in this book are simple practices that can help you strengthen your vagus nerve.

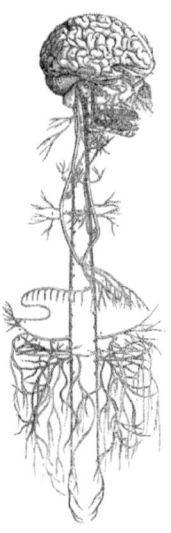

SOMATIC EXERCISES

Somatic exercises consist of performing movement for the pleasure of movement. Throughout the exercise, you focus on your inner experience as you move and expand your internal awareness.

Thomas Hanna, an educator in the field, coined the term in 1970 to describe a number of techniques that share an important similarity: They help people increase their body awareness through a combination of movement and relaxation.

While somatic practices have become increasingly popular in the Western world over the past 50 years, many draw inspiration from ancient Eastern healing philosophy and practices, including tai chi and qi gong.

These exercises can help you learn more efficient ways of moving and replace older, less useful movement patterns.

Unlike traditional workouts, you don't try to squeeze in as many exercises as possible. Instead, you try to perform each exercise in a way that it teaches you something about your body and its movements.

Being more in touch with your body can also have the added benefit of increasing your emotional awareness. Many people who have difficulty expressing difficult emotions find it easier to convey them through movement.

"Somatic" refers to the mind-body connection – the integration of thoughts, emotions and physical sensations.

When we notice something is wrong in our body, it is a sign that our thoughts and emotions also need some attention.

Children are particularly sensitive to their bodily sensations and can often sense when something is wrong long before adults can.

However, they may not have the words to express how they feel or understand how to cope in a healthy way.

This is where somatics comes in!

By learning simple techniques like breathing exercises and gentle movements, you can learn to release tension, reduce stress and improve your overall well-being.

These exercises can help you learn gentler ways of moving and replace tighter, less useful movements.

Unlike traditional workouts, you don't try to do as many repetitions as possible. Instead, you try to perform each exercise in a way that it teaches you something about your body and your movements.

Being more in touch with your body can also have the benefit of increasing your awareness of your emotions. Many people who have difficulty expressing difficult emotions find it easier to convey them through movement and the body.

So let's see in the following pages some particularly effective and easy-to-access somatic exercises.

EMOTION ACCEPTANCE

In somatic exercises, the goal is not to deny your emotions and try to scare them away, to make them go away faster.

The goal is to make room for all emotions, because none are negative and they should all have room to express themselves through your body, so you can let them be and pass.

Through the exercises that you will discover, you will learn to no longer fight against your emotions, you will develop kindness towards yourself and towards others.

You are going to leave room for these emotions, even those that we usually put in the category of emotions that we do not want to feel (anger, fear, stress, sadness, etc.)

You will learn to welcome and observe with curiosity and gentleness what you would usually want to hide under the carpet.
Once you have pointed out this emotion, once you have made it understand that it is OK to be there, it will scare you less and less, and it will be less and less important.

Learning to identify and manage your emotions through somatic practices is essential in a noisy world where you are exposed to many stresses.

Whether it's focusing on breathing exercises, expressing emotions through movement, or understanding the physical effects of emotions, these practices can help you develop healthy coping mechanisms that will be useful throughout your life.

Once you have a flexible and calm nervous system, step 2!

Act!

Decide to move forward towards what is important to you.

Once you learn to switch your nervous system into cool parasympathetic mode, you will be able to use your energy to do what matters to you:

- Being kind and generous with others
- Learning new things
- Taking care of your family etc...
- Taking care of your health
- Travelling
- Going out with friends
- Developing projects, your career
- Playing sports

So let's discover in the following pages some somatic exercises that are particularly effective and simple to do.

ALOHA

When you will be practicing the exercises here, the breathing and the meditation, I would like you to also practice what I call the ALOHA method.
Aloha means in Hawaiian: hello, welcome, goodbye, affection, love, compassion and that's exactly what you will do here!

Each time you will have a strong emotion, a strong thought about something, when you are feeling angry about how you feel, about your illness etc…, when you are feeling sad…
Just start by

A → Accepting

L → Letting go

O → Observing / your thoughts, your body, the tension here and there

H → Hosting / Make space for these feelings to be there, make sure you listen to them

A → Acting / From there, decide what you want to do, what can help, if you can change something, or if you should just let go and change the direction you move to.

MEDICAL DISCLAIMER

This book details the author's personal experiences with and opinions about somatic exercises. The author is not a healthcare provider.

The author and publisher are providing this book and its contents on an "as is" basis and make no representations or warranties of any kind with respect to this book or its contents. The author and publisher disclaim all such representations and warranties, including for example warranties of merchantability and healthcare for a particular purpose. In addition, the author and publisher do not represent or warrant that the information accessible via this book is accurate, complete or current.

They are not intended to diagnose, treat, cure, or prevent any condition or disease. Please consult with your own physician or healthcare specialist regarding the suggestions and recommendations made in this book.

Except as specifically stated in this book, neither the author or publisher, nor any authors, contributors, or other representatives will be liable for damages arising out of or in connection with the use of this book.

This is a comprehensive limitation of liability that applies to all damages of any kind, including (without limitation)

24

compensatory; direct, indirect or consequential damages; loss of data, income or profit; loss of or damage to property and claims of third parties.

You understand that this book is not intended as a substitute for consultation with a licensed healthcare practitioner, such as your physician. Before you begin any healthcare program, or change your lifestyle in any way, you will consult your physician or another licensed healthcare practitioner to ensure that you are in good health and that the examples contained in this book will not harm you.

This book provides content related to physical and/or mental health issues. As such, use of this book implies your acceptance of this disclaimer.

MOVES AND POSES

Now let's start with the exercises!

SHAKING PRACTICE

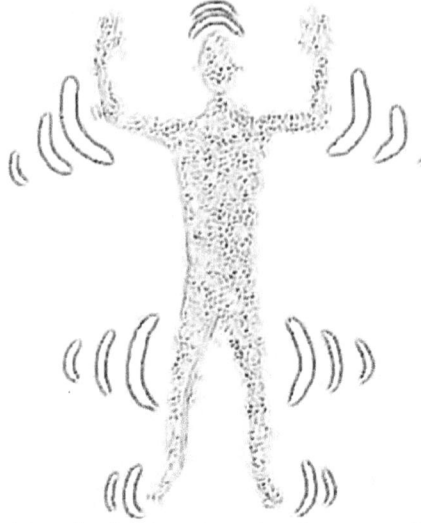

My favorite exercise, one of the most complete and at the same time the simplest, to relax your body and mind in a short time and which you can do anywhere, is shaking the body. It's a simple way to improve your health and well-being.

This simple shake can be done anywhere, just shake the part of the body that feels tense. Jump, kick and shake your hands. Surrender to the jerks. Let out all the sounds that want to come out. You will feel the release of tension.

Visually, it's shaking your body, in every way that's pleasant, to release tension.

We can start by simply shaking the hands, releasing tension in the wrists, leaving the fingers free to move in the direction they want.

We continue by shrugging our shoulders and lowering them several times in a row, while maintaining the movement of the hands and arms.

And so on, we add a shaking of the torso, the buttocks, we can lift one leg then the other to shake them as well.

And we continue this exercise, possibly with music, for a few minutes. You can jump a little, but while maintaining flexibility and lightness, no tension.

You can breathe long sighs during the practice of shaking, it is yet another way to release tension and shift your nervous system to parasympathetic mode.

Shaking is a very powerful practice that can release blockages in the body and have profound healing effects. It really helps clear blocked emotions. Here are some videos you can refer to for a more visual example.

https://www.youtube.com/watch?v=Tx8CVkfmIYE

https://www.youtube.com/watch?v=Xh0ZLeQNfrM

You can also practice shaking sitting or lying down.

You can lie on your back with your legs facing the sky and shake your legs as hard as possible. This can be a good alternative, especially if you are particularly tired after a long day on your feet.

You can then stay for a few minutes with your legs in the air in the posture below, the best is to have your legs propped up against a wall to really let yourself go and breathe deeply.

5 minutes in this position and you will feel regenerated! Relaxation guaranteed!

QI GONG SWING

This simple movement improves circulation, releases tension in your neck and shoulders, and cleanses your lymphatic system.

Start in a standing posture with your arms outstretched in front of you, and swing them back.

As you pump backwards, you can rise onto your tiptoes, and return to flat when your arms are forward. You don't need to, you can stay flat on your feet!

It is recommended to practice it for 15 minutes a day but 3 to 5 is already a good start! It's even better if you can do it outside.

You can keep a slight bend in the knees, and maintain a flexible posture.

TAI CHI TWIST

A slightly different version is to swing your arms right and left, instead of back and forth.

The standing spinal twist is a movement that you can do at will, at any time of the day to relax your muscles, your spine, etc., especially after a long period of sitting.

Here again, we are on a pendulum movement, very soothing for the nervous system.

Start by standing in a neutral position, feet hip-width apart, knees slightly bent.

Stand with your feet shoulder-width apart, arms relaxed at your sides. Pivot at the waist, allowing the arms to swing naturally. Focus on keeping the hips still, pushing the hip forward slightly to counter each twist. Increase the pace as you go; you can intensify the movement if you feel comfortable.

Maintain suppleness, flexibility in your movements, a slight bend in your knees.

You can gently close your eyes to let yourself be lulled by the movement.

Practice for a minimum of 1 minute straight and as long and often as you want! Then come back to center, still, and observe your energy.

This helps release tension in the spine, which is also very pleasant after a long period of sitting, for example, or a long car journey.

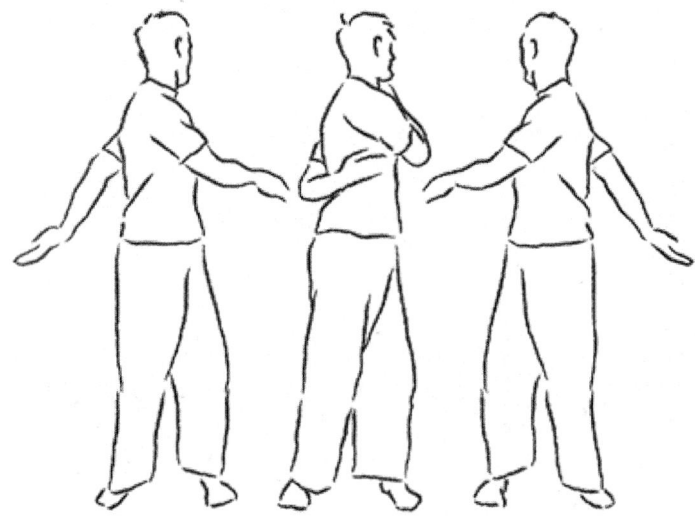

BAMBOO IN THE WIND AND SELF HUG

This rocking motion will help release built-up tension.

Standing with your arms relaxed at your sides, a slight bend in your knees, gently swing back and forth or from right to left like a bamboo in the wind for one minute.

You may also notice small tremors in your body that may seem a little unusual at first but allow tensions to dissolve through you. It's a way for the body to release tension.

Do this for a minute or more.

You can also add to this movement what I call a self-hug, that is to say you hug yourself, as if you were rocking a child, but we will see this exercise more in depth in the next pages.

ROCKING COBRA

The rocking cobra is a movement inspired by the cobra posture.

Just come and lie down on your stomach, on a mat or on your bed.

You slightly lift your torso by supporting yourself on your hands; you can go much lower than in the posture below.

The goal is for it to be comfortable, to stay there for several minutes.

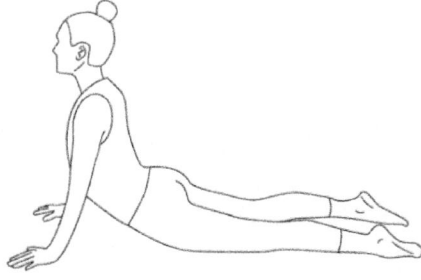

In this posture, we will then swing the hips from right to left, as if we wanted to rock this cobra.

You can also do this hip swing with your forehead resting on your forearms for an additional level of relaxation.

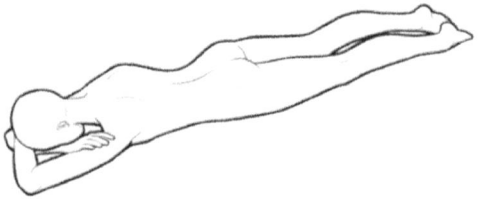

You can rock more or less quickly depending on the sensations of the moment.

The ideal is to practice 2 to 3 minutes continuously, at the end of the day to relax for example.

Try to go as slowly as possible and use as little effort as possible.

All of this is a great way to bring you into a deeper state of parasympathetic dominance – to allow you to feel calm and grounded. Bonus points if you can hum while you swing, because humming helps stimulate the vagus nerve.

Rocking stimulates the relaxation response, while gently relaxing the muscles along the spine sends additional signals to the brain that you are safe and able to relax. Add to that deep breathing and you have a complete formula for rebalancing your nervous system.

ROCKING HAPPY BABY

Continuing from the previous movement and in the same logic, we find a posture, which here becomes a movement that can be repeated as often as necessary.

This is the happy baby posture, which will here be combined with a rocking movement.

The same type of swing as for the rocked cobra pose, but potentially an even more relaxing posture, since you are lying on your back.

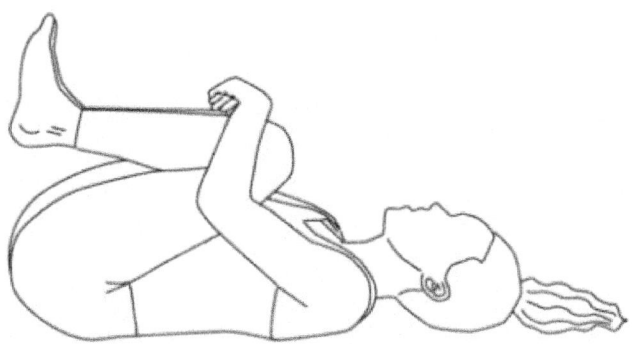

In this posture, the idea is to initiate a swing from right and left, possibly also from front to back, light, without excessive effort, to be able to prolong the movement as long as necessary.

You can also put a blanket on yourself to feel even more peaceful and relaxed at the end.

Here again, as in the previous posture, adding deep abdominal breathing, and soft sounds like hhhuuuummmm, and long sighs, can still help the nervous system to relax further.

You can grab your knees and make circles with your lower back. Stretch one leg and then the other to create a little momentum so that you increase your range of motion without using energy.

We also find in this posture the principle of the self-hug.

SITTED PENDULUM

Once again a very simple and very powerful exercise.

You can also place your hands on your shoulders rather than behind your head, this is another variation.

I call this movement the sitting pendulum, because it swings from right to left like a pendulum.

Sit on the floor with your legs bent or on a chair with your feet anchored in the ground, so that you have enough room to the right and left to lean sideways.

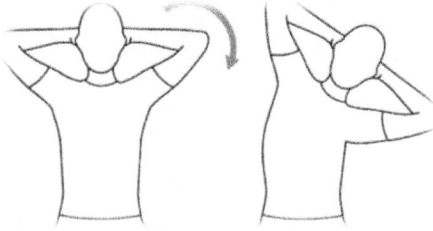

Place your hands on your shoulders, elbows spread to the sides, you can also put your hands behind your head.

You will then simply lean to the right then to the left, slowly, in a pendulum movement.

And you repeat this movement while breathing deeply for 1 to 2 minutes.

Rocking movements in general help calm the nervous system, so it's an ideal movement to practice if you're feeling sad or anxious.

This is an opportunity to open up to your emotions, let yourself cry while you rock, if you feel the need. This type of movement can also cause yawning, and that's a very good sign! This means that your nervous system relaxes and you go into parasympathetic mode!

ROCKING ON ALL FOURS

"Rocking" is one of the most complete movements. It nourishes your nervous system and teaches your body and all its limbs how to move fluidly, together, as one unit.

In doing so, the body learns rhythm, coordination, stability and mobility. In other words, the body learns to move the way it was designed to move.

Another wonderful benefit of rocking is that it helps restore adult posture. It can even help relieve lower back pain by releasing the lower back, restoring mobility to this area.

When all joints move freely and in unison, the brain feels safe enough to remove any limitations it may have placed on the body. Limitations such as pain, stiffness, and weakness often disappear when the brain knows where everything is in the body. Swinging lets the brain know where everything is!

Another wonderful benefit of swinging is that in addition to uniting the whole body in a beautiful physical flow, it unites the whole person, inside and out. Swinging calms the mind. When the brain feels safe, when it obtains all the information it is looking for, the nervous system finds itself in the parasympathetic state, at rest, digestion, fulfillment, smiling and well-being. When the brain feels safe, emotions and thoughts will also be peaceful and relaxed. Swinging is a fantastic way to literally wash away your worries, melt away tension from your body and stress from your mind.

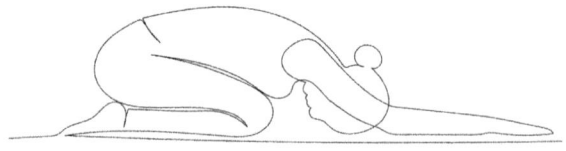

Try this 1-3 times a day, every day, for 3 minutes at a time:

Get on all fours.

Inhale through your nose and exhale through your nose or mouth.

Rock gently back and forth by swinging your hips toward your feet, then rock your body forward on your hands.

Explore different foot positions, different leg spacing and pelvic openings. Go slow or faster, you can also try to stretch to the sides, do circles...

EXPLORE, be gentle and curious. Don't be aggressive.

You don't need to go that low on your heels!!

Just initiate the rocking motion slowly and see where you go from there.

This swinging motion might be one of the best movements you can do to help you feel good in your body, your mind. It's one of the few moves with incredible power potential to help you live your life better.

CHAIR TO RELEASE LOWER BACK

Sometimes stress can cause pain, blockages and unpleasant sensations in the lower back.

To decompress your lower back, give yourself a little more space in this area, you can adopt the following posture for a few breaths.

Assume the pose called chair pose, which means you bend your knees, as if you want to sit in an imaginary chair.

You can swing a little to the right and left, undulate, to find a pleasant posture.

Then place your hands firmly on your thighs and apply firm pressure on them so as to stretch the spine.

You should feel a feeling of warmth and space in your lower back.

You can stay here for a minute, breathing deeply.

Coming out of the posture, make a few small shaking movements to restart blood circulation in the legs.

Repeat as many times as necessary, especially after sitting for a long time, at work or in the car.

TREE IN THE WIND

The tree pose is one of the best-known balance postures.

Being balanced in your body is essential to having a feeling of stability. Tree pose can help improve the strength of the muscles that help you stay upright and balanced. The arms extended in this pose help engage the muscles that control the position of the torso.

This posture can particularly engage the ankle muscles to provide better balance and also improve blood circulation.

This posture can be beneficial in calming the entire nervous system, causing a feeling of relaxation.

This can be helpful in improving proprioception ability, which is the ability to sense body movement, position, and action.

It also helps improve concentration, generate calm and balance the nervous system.

Due to this effect, it can help with conditions such as depression and anxiety.

Start standing

Bend your right knee and place the sole of your right foot against your left thigh.

Move your hands toward your hips for balance.

Make sure your supporting leg foot is pointing straight forward.

Keep your hips square and avoid rotating your pelvis.

Pull your right knee back as far as you can while keeping your hips square.

While holding your legs like this, raise your arms outwards and upwards until your palms touch above your head.

Hold for 5 to 10 breaths.

You can then move your shaft, bringing the knee of the lifted leg forward, then out to the side again, to open the hip.

You can also move your arms to the sides.

Imagine that you are a tree in the wind, and that the breath of it makes your branches move delicately.

LEG SWINGS

This is an ideal movement to relax the psoas.

A contracted psoas signals this state of stress to the body, and ultimately, the consequence is exhaustion of the adrenal glands and the immune system (with all the physical phenomena associated with stress that we know).

Due to an excessive number of hours spent in a seated position (in front of the computer, in front of the TV, in transport, etc.), a lack of physical activity or a lack of stretching after sport, psychological trauma that has been accumulating for years... in many of us the psoas is perpetually contracted, inevitably ending up shortening due to this tension which curls up on it.

The leg swing is a quick solution that will make your hips feel light and free and will soften the psoas area.

To do this, all you need is something to stand on, like a block, a staircase, a small stool, or whatever you have nearby.

Take a block or a thick book and place it 30cm from a wall. Stand on the block or book with your left foot, supporting and balancing with your right hand on the wall. Let your right leg and foot hang completely relaxed. Gently swing this leg back and forth like a pendulum, taking care not to let the trunk bend or twist as your leg swings. (If your pelvis contracts, you are exceeding the free range of motion of your psoas.) See if you can feel the pendulum movement deep in your torso. This should start at the very top of your psoas, at your 12th thoracic vertebra, behind your solar plexus.

Don't try to go as high as in the picture below!

After swinging the leg for a few minutes, step off the block and see if your two legs feel different. You have released the psoas attached to the swinging leg and that leg will most likely be longer, freer and more relaxed.

Now reverse your position and swing the other leg. This time, focus not only on the leg you're swinging, but also the standing leg. Make sure you are not leaning over the hip of the standing leg. Try to feel your weight pass directly through your leg and foot and into the block. Even though this leg is now bearing weight, you can relax the psoas by shifting your attention to the front of the hip and relieving any tension you notice there.

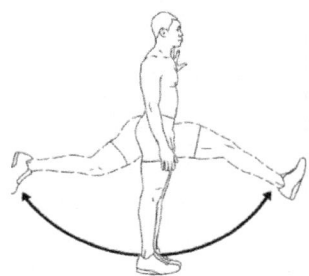

Invite the swinging leg to be heavy when you swing it.

Make sure you are swinging from your thigh and not your knee.

Enjoy the movement for a minute or more.

Before switching legs, step off the block and once you have both feet on the ground, notice the sensation of one side in relation to the other.

I hope you enjoy this super simple but super effective leg swing for the hips and psoas.

And the psoas being one of the places where stress is most lodged, that's why it is also beneficial to relax it!

SELF HUGS

Hugs can bring a lot of comfort.

They can help you feel closer to someone you care about, whether it's a partner, friend, or child. They can also increase feelings of happiness and fulfillment by strengthening your knowledge that others care about you.

When circumstances prevent you from spending time with loved ones, you may feel desperately craving physical affection. Touch is a basic need, so it's completely normal. Going without it, especially for a longer period of time than usual, can have a pretty big impact on your emotional health.

In the meantime, if you really need a hug and you're alone, why not try giving yourself one?

Self-hugs may seem a little awkward, even silly, but they are very effective.

The importance of human connections cannot be understated, and social support provides many benefits. For example, when someone you love puts their arms around you to hold you, you probably feel comforted and less alone.

Hugging can replicate these feelings of comfort and security. Think of it as a sort of stand-in until you can kiss someone else again.

You play the most important role in your own well-being, and hugging yourself can help you remember your power. Instead of waiting for someone else to support you and help you feel better, you can take steps to comfort yourself.

Touch, even your own touch, helps promote relaxation because it reduces levels of cortisol (the stress hormone) in your body. Of course, a hug won't solve your problems entirely, but it can help relieve some of your tension and stress.

So the next time you're feeling exhausted or irritable, taking the time to give a nice, long hug can help lift your spirits and brighten your mood.

Practicing kindness towards yourself helps you accept yourself more easily as you are and calm down after trials or mistakes. By increasing conscious acceptance and self-esteem, self-compassion can also improve your overall outlook on life.

How to do?

Bend your arms around your body, positioning them naturally and comfortably. For example, crossing your arms over your stomach or just below your chest may seem easier than hugging your chest.

Place your hands on your shoulders or upper arm (just above your biceps). Again, go with what feels natural to you. If you're hugging yourself on your stomach, you may find it comfortable to curl your hands around your sides.

Imagine the type of hug you want. A strong and intense hug? Or a softer, soothing hug?

Squeeze with just enough pressure to create the sensation you're looking for.

Hold the hug for as long as you want.

Some people find it soothing to gently rock back and forth while hugging, so you might also consider trying this method.

If you don't feel like hugging, try stroking your forearms or upper shoulders in a soothing way, similar to a gentle massage.

53

WHIRLING DERVISH

The whirling dervish is one of my favorite exercises. When I
do this exercise, I feel my entire upper body open, stretch,
relax and release tension. All internal organs get a great
massage (it's great if you're a little constipated!) and the deep
breathing totally cleanses and refreshes our system. Three
minutes is enough for a total mental, emotional and energetic
reset! It's incredible.

The benefits are numerous:

Stretches the fascia, massages the viscera, opens the heart
region, works on the lymph in the chest, throat and under the
armpits, massages the spine, back muscles and hips.

A slow and sensual posture that mobilizes the whole body.

A radical dose of self-love

They are also said to positively influence the adrenal glands, which help manage the stress response.

For this exercise, start in an easy seated posture, with your legs crossed. The torso then moves in circles around the midline, inhaling as the body moves forward and exhaling backward. Typically, they are performed clockwise first, then counterclockwise, for up to three minutes on each side.

Grasp your knees firmly and begin moving your spine in a clockwise circular motion. Imagine drawing a circle around yourself with your chin. Inhale while leaning forward and exhale while leaning back.

HIP CIRCLES

Hip circles are a great dynamic stretching exercise. This exercise helps loosen the muscles in your lower back and hips, strengthen the core, and slim the waist.

It is also a great exercise to relieve stress and tension and improve your flexibility.

The hips are an important storage tank for emotional stress due to the connection between the psoas and the adrenal glands and the location of the sacral chakra, if chakra stories speak to you.

When you're stressed, your emotional and physical health can suffer. People suffering from trauma, stress, or mental illnesses such as anxiety and depression often experience physical symptoms as well. In all of this, there is perhaps one common link: the hips. Neuroscience indicates that the hips are a potential reservoir for storing emotions.

The psoas muscle, located in the lower back and connected to the hip joint, is particularly sensitive to tension and trauma. When you experience a traumatic event, your body may instinctively contract and tighten the psoas muscle to protect itself. Over time, this tension can become chronic and lead to a range of physical and emotional symptoms.

Symptoms of stored trauma to the hips can vary widely, but may include:

- Chronic pain or stiffness in the hips or lower back
- Difficulty relaxing or feeling comfortable during hip openers
- Feelings of anxiety, depression, or emotional numbness
- Difficulty expressing emotions or feeling creative

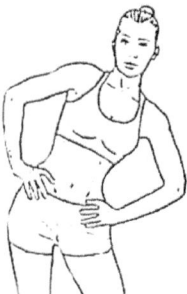 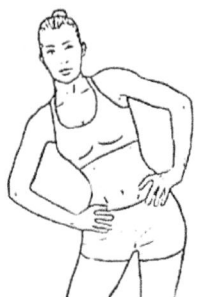

The movement is quite simple to understand.

Spread your legs hip-width apart, and begin to make circles with your pelvis, back and forth, more or less quickly depending on the desire and need of the moment.

3 minutes is a good length of time to relax the pelvis. You must of course practice the circles in one direction then the other. It is also a good exercise to do when you wake up to get your muscles and joints started.

PILLOW SLAMS

One of the most effective exercises for angry people!

Very easy to do too, you just need to have a cushion or pillow available.

The Pillow Slam in English aims to release the frustration and anger stored inside you.

Find a cushion

Raise it above your head and slam it to the ground.

Release extra energy by standing on your tiptoes or adding a bounce when you slap the pillow.

Repeat until you run out of energy or until you notice your body shaking or shuddering.

Bring your hands to your heart and connect to your body.

You might feel a strong emotional release while doing this exercise. Let this emotion flow through your body. Repeat the pillow throw if necessary.

SHOULDER SHRUGS AND HEEL DROPS

During a stressful day, we can often feel our shoulders starting to lift towards our ears: we tend to have a lot of tension in the trapezius muscles.

It's always good to remember to relax the shoulders or let the shoulder blades slide down the back, but sometimes you need something a little stronger to get the trapezius muscles to let go.

I have the move you need: a shrug with a strong, powerful release/drop. It may seem a little strange to intentionally shrug your shoulders when they're already tense, but putting the muscle under full tension and then fully relaxing will help your body notice when tension is creeping in and make it easier to release the tension.

All of this can even reduce the feeling of stress by alleviating one of the physical symptoms. (It's a bit like very targeted progressive muscle relaxation.)

Start standing, sitting or kneeling. Hold a proud chest, shoulders back and down.

Inhale and shrug your shoulders as high as possible towards your ears.

Exhale and let the shoulders fall forcefully back into place. I recommend letting the air escape your lungs with an audible sigh – a very loud, very slow exhale.

Perform a few shrugs and release until you are ready to move on.

I like to add a little bonus to this movement. When you shrug your shoulders as high as possible, you can also rise on your tiptoes. And when you relax your shoulders, you can let yourself fall heavily on your heels, a total relaxation, and at the same time a complete vibration of the body which brings it back to a neutral state.

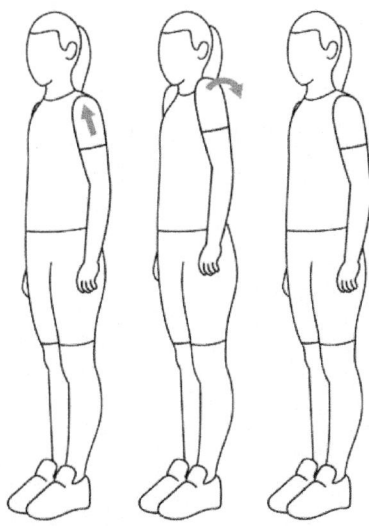

HIP OPENER POSES

As stress causes your body to contract, the hips become essential for nurturing and relieving emotional tension.

In the holistic wellness community, teachers will often talk about "storing emotions in our hips." Therefore, many yogis use hip-opening exercises to regulate emotions.

Many believe that the hips hold our tension because they are located near the sacral chakra, a key energy center associated with emotions and connection.

At the same time, more than 20 muscles run through the hip region, closely linked to your stress response. Therefore, when your hips are tight, sore and neglected, it affects the entire body. Some hip-opening exercises and stretches target specific muscles in this area, improving circulation, energy, movement and even reducing back pain. Therefore, as stress causes your body to contract, the hips become crucial for nurturing and relieving emotional tension.

As you experiment with these hip-opening stretches, try to approach them with self-compassion. This movement can bring to the surface emotions and thoughts that you weren't expecting. Dealing with this will likely be difficult for some people, and I encourage you to stay present with every sensation and emotion that arises.

It's essential to move at your own pace and not force your muscles into positions that cause pain, especially if you're new to hip opening or have a condition that limits mobility.

Here are five exercises to open your hips:

1. PIGEON POSE

A popular pose offering a deep stretch to the thighs, back, groin, piriformis and psoas.

The easiest way to get into pigeon pose is to start on all 4 legs.

The knees should be placed under the hips, and the hands are placed under the shoulders.

Bring your left knee forward by sliding it, place the shin diagonally to the chest so that the knee is almost in contact with the left wrist, and the foot is close to the right hand.

Slide your right leg back, with your knee straight and your thigh pressed to the floor. Lower the left buttock to sit on it. If you are flexible enough, you can bend your left leg to its maximum so that you can sit on your heel. In all cases, be sure to keep your pelvis forward.

Once in position, begin to breathe deeply, emphasizing the exhalation time.

You can place a cushion or folded blanket under your hip to make this pose more comfortable. You can slowly lean forward as you strike the pose. Focus on your breathing and the different sensations that come from it – emotional, mental or physical.

2. LIZARD POSE OR LOW LUNGE

Lizard pose, also known as gecko pose, focuses on the hips, groin, and inner hamstrings. This pose allows for an intense stretch, but I recommend trying a variation if you're still developing your flexibility. If you enjoyed Lizard pose, a similar hip-opening pose to try is a low lunge. Again, downward facing dog is a suitable starting point. When you're ready, place one foot toward the outside of your hand. Make sure your knee is at a 90-degree angle and positioned above the ankle. Hold this pose for a few deep, slow breaths before repeating it on the other side.

If tight hips make it difficult to lower your forearms, that's okay! Practice with your hands on the floor, and when you're ready, use blocks or a pillow to slowly lower over time as your hips gain mobility.

Use a cushion under the back knee to relieve any discomfort and avoid too much pressure on the kneecap. You can roll the outside of your mat inwards or place a blanket under the back knee.

Keep the neck long, relaxed and aligned with the rest of the spine. Avoid lowering your head.

Breathe slowly and deeply to release tension. Relax your jaw as you exhale with a long, deep sigh.

3. RECLINING TWIST

This posture is ideal for relieving stress because it targets the glutes, chest and obliques. This pose doesn't focus on the hips as much as the others but offers an "opening heart" position.

Many use this posture to "flush" the body and allow emotions to flow. To deepen this stretch and make it work for you, make sure you don't hold your breath. Instead, take a deep breath and accept where your body is in this position, whether your knee touches the ground or not.

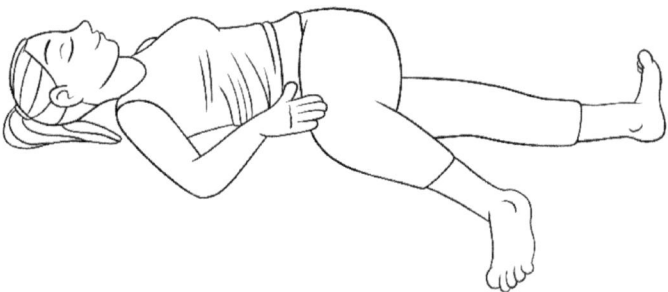

Twists are a great way to decompress and release anxiety and frustrations from your day, just like wringing out a sponge. They also stimulate and detoxify the organs in your torso. If you've ever felt exhausted at the end of a workday or after a weekend of excessive fun, this pose is a great pose to help restore balance.

To begin, lie on your back with your knees bent and your feet flat on the floor. You can rest your head on a pillow or blanket for additional neck support. Let your arms rest at your sides.

As you exhale, bring both knees toward your chest and clasp your hands around them. This is the knee-to-chest pose.

Extend your left leg along the floor, keeping your right knee pulled toward your chest. Extend your right arm along the floor at shoulder height, palm facing down.

Shift your hips slightly to the right. Next, place your left hand on the outside of your right knee. As you exhale, drop your right knee to the left side of your body. Keep your left hand placed gently on your right knee.

Turn your head to the right. Soften your gaze toward the tip of your right finger. Keep your shoulder blades pressed toward the floor and away from your ears. Let the force of gravity bring your knee even closer to the ground. If your right toes can touch the ground, let your foot rest.

Hold the pose for 10 to 25 breaths. On an inhale, slowly return to center, bringing both knees toward your chest in Knees to Chest Pose.

Exhale and extend your right leg along the floor. Repeat steps on opposite side.

When you have finished the pose, hug your knees to your chest for a few breaths in Knee to Chest Pose.

Then exhale slowly while extending both legs on the floor.

4. SITTED BUTTERFLY

This stretch provides a cleansing motion for your hips. Start
seated with your spine straight and shoulders relaxed. By
bringing the soles of your feet together, opening your legs,
and letting gravity pull your knees down, your hips receive a
deep, slow stretch. The "Butterfly Stretch" will target the
inner thighs, hips, lower back and groin. Don't force your legs
down; instead, let them open gently while you focus on deep
breathing.

Start in a seated position with your spine straight and legs
apart.

Bend your knees and bring your feet towards your pelvis

The soles of your feet should touch each other

Grasp your feet firmly with your hands (you can place your hands under your feet for support)

Make an effort to bring your heels as close to your groin as possible without straining.

Inhale deeply

As you exhale, lean forward and press your thighs and knees toward the floor.

Make a slight effort to continue to press your thighs downward

Start flapping both legs up and down like a butterfly's wings for 30 seconds to a minute.

Start slowly and gradually increase the speed, continue breathing normally

Inhale deeply and, as you exhale, lean forward, keeping your chin raised with your spine straight.

Support your elbows on your thighs or knees, bringing your knees and thighs closer to the floor.

Feel the stretch in your inner thighs and take long, deep breaths, relaxing the muscles more and more.

Inhale deeply and raise your chest

As you exhale, gently relax the posture. Straighten your legs in front of you and relax

5. THREAD THE NEEDLE

Needle Eye Pose is a restorative hip opener that goes by many names, such as Lying Pigeon or Knee to Ankle Pose.

It's a gentler alternative to Pigeon Pose for those who want to work on opening tight hips, and works much better for those with tender or injured knees.

In the somatic style, you can sway right and left, back and forth, and breathe deeply into the movement.

Lie on your back. Bend your knees and place your feet on the floor.

Bring your bent left leg closer to your chest and hug it.

Then move the leg so that the left ankle rests on top of the right thigh, just above the knee.

Open the left knee to the side.

Now put the left hand between the legs and meet it with the right hand behind the right. Alternatively, you can also tie them around the right shin.

Bring your thighs towards you until you feel a stretching sensation. Flex your feet and keep your lower back on the floor.

Hold the position for 5 to 10 deep breaths, or between 3 and 5 minutes for the Yin version of the pose. Release and repeat on the other side.

SEATED FORWARD BEND

The seated forward bend is a calming posture with many benefits for the body and mind. This posture provides an intense stretch of the hamstrings and spine.

This posture is a universal recovery posture for many other physical activities. Let's bend and stretch together!

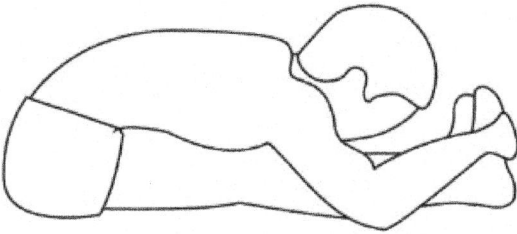

This posture calms the mind while bringing awareness inward.

It helps relieve stress, anxiety, headaches. This posture also stimulates the liver and kidneys while facilitating digestion!

Sit on the floor with your legs extended in front of you.

Press your palms or fingertips on the floor next to your hips to lengthen your spine.

Lean forward from the hip joints, not the waist.

Keep the spine long as the torso tilts forward over the legs.

You can keep a slight bend at the knees. Here again this is not a competition for flexibility. The objective is to accept being where we are, without forcing. Kindness and compassion! It doesn't need to look like the picture over there!

Place hands on shins, ankles, outside of feet, or on the floor alongside the legs.

With each inhale, lift and lengthen the spine, pulling the chest forward.

With each exhalation, release a little more completely into the forward bend.

Let the lower stomach, ribs and then chest rest on the top of the thighs.

Stay in this pose for 5 to 10 breaths.

You can flex your knees and you don't need to force at all!

Even in this pose, don't feel stuck.

Here too you create your own move, flex your knees, oscillate right and left, forward and back.

Breathe deeply into it, sigh, hum, make noises.

I am repeating myself but these are the real tools, this is where the letting go happens.

Stop the fight and let go.

Don't try to make the perfect pose or a good looking move.

Don't worry about what others may think about you or what you look like. Just enjoy the place where you are.

To exit, extend your chest forward and inhale as you move up a long spine.

This calming effect occurs thanks to your spine, which is like a channel between your brain and the rest of your body. The forward clamp stretches and creates space between the vertebrae of the spine, which controls our autonomic nervous system. This system directly affects our response to stress.

When you're in a bent posture, you also create space for better circulation in your spinal cord, which sends a calming signal to your brain.

The seated forward bend is a quick way to get out of fight/flight mode and go in the rest and digest mode.

THE BUTTERFLY BRIDGE (TRE EXERCISE)

TRE (Tension and Trauma Releasing Exercises) is a practice in its own right that would require an entire book to give it enough space. You will find books on the subject, if it is a theme that interests you.

The principle of the TRE method lies in triggering the natural mechanism of "neurogenic" tremors by doing a series of 7 exercises. It should be noted that these exercises are simple, accessible to everyone (children, adults, athletes, seniors, etc.). They are designed to stretch, stimulate or fatigue the muscles that inhibit tremors. They also prepare the body and ground it. When the tremors are triggered during the last phase of the exercises (in a lying position), it remains to let them develop little by little and do their work of relaxation for around ten minutes. The exercises most often first produce tremors in the thighs. They will cause tremors up to the psoas, release tensions in the sacrum and via the spine will reach the nape of the neck and the base of the skull. Activation of tremors allows you to quickly relax the psoas in a non-intrusive manner.

Once the technique is learned and mastered, after several sessions, the warm-up exercises can be accelerated or replaced with your usual exercises such as walking or fitness. The technique then becomes a quick and effective method of relaxation. Eventually, these tremors may occur on their own when you are in a resting position. Your body will naturally act to reduce the stress or tension you have accumulated during the day. Be careful though, for some people, doing the exercises alone is not enough. In this case, it is necessary to be able to be accompanied by a trained practitioner.

One of the advantages of this method is that the body resolves the effects of trauma on its own without the need to speak or remember specific events. One of the main reasons people don't want to work through their trauma is because they are forced to talk about events and experiences or relive the feelings and emotions that overwhelmed them at the time. Here, since neurogenic tremors are an automatic bodily process, it is not useful to use words to release tension.

One of the objectives of the T.R.E® method is to teach people to self-regulate vibrations safely so that they are able to regain control of their body physiology and gradually return to a peaceful balance.

Here we are only going to see an exercise that I call the Butterfly Bridge

Lie on your back with your knees bent.

Bring the soles of your feet together and let your knees fall sideways toward the floor.

Bend your elbows and press them against the floor for stability.

Press your lower back against the floor.

Squeeze your butt together and push your hips up into the air.

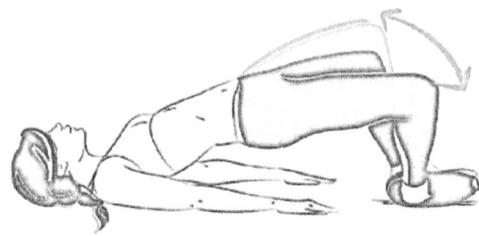

Your body forms a sort of bridge, hence the name of this exercise.

Stay in the position for a few breaths, you can let your glutes oscillate from right to left, make gentle movements in all directions, go down a little, come back up.

The goal is to wait until tremors appear in your legs, and possibly your spine. To do this you can also try to bring your knees together very gently, until you find a point where the tremors will start.

Then the objective is to accept your tremors, not to try to control them or to master yourself, but to let them be, to let go, and to stay like this for 3 to 5 minutes, as much as is bearable and relatively comfortable.

You can then relax the posture, gently place your lower back on the ground, bring your knees to your chest, and make a few circles here, before lying down completely on your back to benefit from the relaxing effects of this exercise.

BUTTERFLY HUG

The Butterfly Hug technique is a simple yet potent self-help tool that can be used to alleviate anxiety, stress, and emotional distress. It falls under the category of bilateral stimulation, which involves activating both sides of the body to stimulate the brain and promote relaxation. This technique can be employed in various situations, such as when you're feeling overwhelmed, experiencing panic attacks, or simply seeking a moment of calm in your daily life.

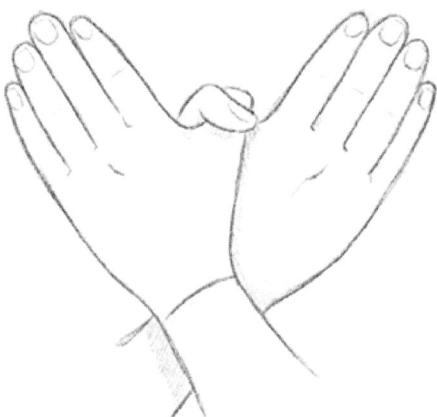

To reap the benefits of the Butterfly Hug, follow these simple steps:

Find a comfortable position: Sit in a chair or find a quiet spot where you can relax and focus.

Cross your arms: Gently cross your arms over your chest, placing your hands on your upper arms or shoulders.

Start tapping: Begin a gentle, rhythmic tapping motion with your hands, alternating between your left and right sides. The motion should feel like a gentle butterfly landing on your arms.

Breathe deeply: As you tap, take slow, deep breaths in through your nose and out through your mouth. Allow your breath to flow naturally, bringing a sense of calm and relaxation with each exhale.

Focus on your emotions: While performing the Butterfly Hug, direct your attention to the emotions or sensations you're experiencing. Acknowledge them without judgment, allowing yourself to fully embrace the present moment.

Continue for several minutes: Repeat the tapping motion and deep breathing for at least five to ten minutes, or until you feel a noticeable shift in your emotional state.

The Butterfly Hug technique offers a valuable and accessible tool for achieving emotional well-being and calmness in your daily life. By following the step-by-step instructions outlined in this article, you can harness the power of bilateral stimulation and unlock a profound sense of tranquility. Incorporate this technique into your self-care routine, and experience the transformative effects it can have on your mind and body.

Remember, practice is key. As you consistently implement the Butterfly Hug technique, you will become more proficient in managing stress, regulating your emotions, and finding moments of peace and serenity amidst the demands of everyday life. Embrace this powerful technique, and discover the immense benefits it can bring to your overall well-being.

FRICTION, MASSAGE OF THE WHOLE BODY

You probably already know how a professional massage can help reduce stress, relieve pain and muscle tension. What you may not know is that you can experience the same benefits at home by practicing self-massage, exchanging massages with a loved one, or using a bed or chair with a built-in massage function.

Try taking a few minutes to massage yourself at your desk between tasks, on the couch at the end of a busy day, or in bed to help you relax before bed. To enhance relaxation, you can use an aromatic oil, scented lotion, or combine self-massage with mindfulness or deep breathing techniques.

A combination of movements works well to relieve muscle tension. Try flicking with the edges of your hands or tapping with your fingers or cupped palms. Apply pressure with your fingertips to the muscle knots. Knead the muscles and try long, light, sliding movements. You can apply these movements to any part of the body. Alternate movements of friction, tapping, caressing...The goal is to regain awareness of the limits of your body, to "reinhabit" it.

Think about your legs too, which are often forgotten, your buttocks etc...

For a short session, try focusing on your neck and head:

Start by kneading the neck and shoulder muscles. Form a loose fist and drum quickly up and down the sides and back of your neck. Next, use your thumbs to draw small circles around the base of your skull. Slowly massage the rest of your scalp with your fingertips. Then tap your fingers against your scalp, moving from front to back and then to the sides.

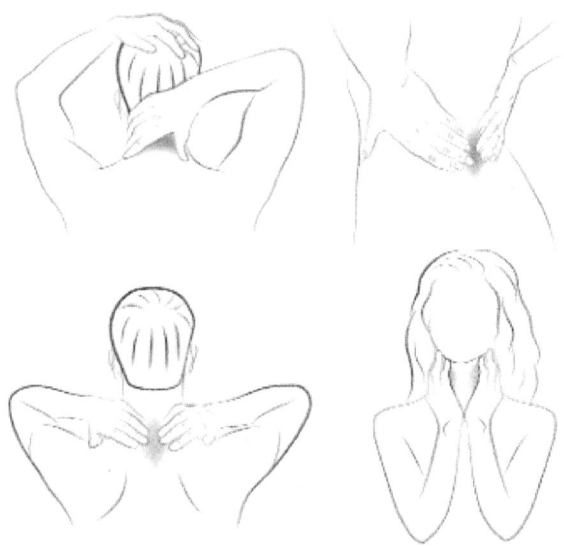

Now massage your face. Make a series of small circles with your thumbs or fingertips. Pay special attention to the muscles in your temples, forehead, and jaw. Use your middle finger to massage the bridge of your nose and work outward across your eyebrows to your temples.

Finally, close your eyes. Cup your hands over your eyes and gently inhale and exhale for a short while.

CLAP YOUR HANDS!

It sounds a little weird, but you'll be surprised to know that clapping and clapping your hands has major health benefits.

To be honest, the benefits of clapping your hands are not limited to physical health benefits but also improve your mental well-being.

The activity of clapping your hands can be done early in the morning to reap many benefits. It is a powerful mental and physical stimulant, as it improves blood circulation in the body. Plus, it acts as a positive affirmation and engages your body as well.

It's an easy activity that can be done by anyone, regardless of age and fitness level.

The Psychological and Behavioral Science International Journal also endorses the mental health benefits of clapping.

This brings positivity because in many cultures, clapping is considered a symbol and gesture of celebration, recognition, praise, encouragement. Whether playing a sport or attending a performance, clapping is used to denote a positive response.

This engages your whole body.

You may notice that clapping does not only involve the hands. Whole body energy is activated during the process of clapping, which automatically improves mood and elevates energy.

Here's the right way to clap.

Sit up straight. You can sit normally and even do this while standing, dancing, etc.

Now raise your arms sideways. Your forearm and fingers should be pointing toward the sky, forming a 90-degree angle with your upper arm and shoulders.

Open your palms wide, keep your upper body tense and straight, and clap. Try to make a very nice CLAP sound.

And repeat. Continue to breathe while moving your arms. If your palm feels hot, don't worry. This is because it happens when blood circulation increases.

So whether you're happy or not, clap! Do this for 1 to 2 minutes when you feel a little tired and you will quickly feel the difference!

RUB YOUR HANDS

Similar to clapping, hand rubbing is a hand movement where the palms are rubbed vigorously against each other.

It is an exercise that can be practiced at any time of the day by anyone.

Rubbing your hands creates heat in the palms.

After hand rubbing, warm palms are placed over the eyes, face, chest, navel, or crown of the head.

After rubbing the palms, when placed on the eyes, the heat soothes stressed eyes and increases blood circulation around the eyes.

This movement creates positive energy in the mind.

Sit in a simple posture with your spine straight.

Keep your shoulders relaxed and breathe a few times.

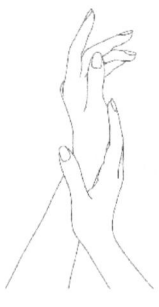

Then start rubbing the palms vigorously so that warmth is felt on the inner side of both palms due to the friction.

Rub vigorously for one or two minutes.

Now place them on the eyes, face and entire body. It calms the mind and body. Repeat this as many times as necessary and inhale deeply, placing them over your eyes.

To repeat at will!

TIGER GROWL

Why do wild animals, which are regularly threatened, bounce back from threats with little or no after-effects? Animals make no judgment on emotions: they simply and very naturally express the bodily response to a real or perceived threat activated by their autonomic nervous system. So why, as animals in our modern world, do we so often struggle to express our emotional response to stressful events? This is what we have been taught to do and it is slowly killing us. Unprocessed emotions also have a societal impact: we often kill each other with repressed, toxic, impulsive anger, also known as rage.

Current studies on mental health suggest that repressing emotions, particularly anger, has a profound impact on our bodies' ability to protect us from disease, including autoimmune diseases such as multiple sclerosis, type 1 diabetes, IBS and rheumatoid arthritis. , as well as chronic fatigue syndrome, fibromyalgia and cancer.

How can emotions cause illness?

Physiologically, emotions are themselves electrical, chemical and hormonal discharges of the human nervous system. When emotions are repressed, this inhibition disarms the body's defenses against illness. The repression of emotions disorganizes our physiological defenses so that instead of protecting us, these defenses become the destroyers of our health.

So how do we express healthy anger so that it doesn't kill us?

Healthy boundaries are part of expressing healthy anger. Boundaries are a way to express our inner defense and send the message to ourselves and others that we matter. When we don't express our needs, when we feel like we're not being heard, or when our needs are simply not met, we build up resentment, which is a toxic form of anger that causes a stress response in our body, which can cause discomfort.

Beyond setting healthy boundaries, it is also necessary to release the primitive response of anger so that it does not accumulate toxicity in our body. Expressing healthy anger is as simple as reverting to our natural animal reactions: a good, healthy, conscious growl. Yes, a good old growl!!

Expressing this animal response sends the message to our nervous system and our primitive brain (the amygdala) that we can – and will – protect ourselves. The growl should be conscious – a slow, engaged expression of anger – like what a tiger would do. He gets into position, engages the muscles of his body, bares his teeth and from his stomach, grunts as he exhales. Try it for yourself and notice what's going on inside. It's a harmless way to naturally release pent-up anger and reduce the stress response in your body.

"Tiger Growling" is a somatic practice that helps release anger from the body.

Inhale and spread your arms out to the side and make your fingers your "claws."

Exhale and slowly bring your arms together. This will be an extremely slow movement in which you create resistance in your muscles, as if you are moving against water. Bonus points if your muscles start to shake!

Let out a low groan as you bring your hands together. The growl must be coming from deep in your belly!

Repeat as many times as necessary!

You can also start the movement in a Warrior position, take a deep breath while leaning back, and exhale with a deep grunt, which comes from the belly, and tilt forward, hands forward as well.

You can even add arm and hand movements, as if you want to scratch your imaginary prey, let off steam, let out your anger!

FIRE GODDESS

Practicing the Goddess is the opportunity to strengthen your legs, your glutes and your abdominals and also your willpower!

It stretches all the muscles of your hips and groin and thus deepens your flexibility. It also develops your balance and allows you to focus on muscular endurance. The posture invites you to benefit from the "goddess" or "god" in you, through its beauty, its strength and its symmetry.

It will require a certain symmetry and great mental and physical stability from you! Deep, conscious breathing will be essential to maintain balance. It will allow you to focus on your alignment.

95

It is also an exercise that works like an inner compass to detect any possible imbalance in your center of gravity and your hips.

Moreover, you will feel the difficulty of standing straight if everything is not aligned in the posture. This imbalance in your hips, shoulders, back and upper body will be felt very quickly. Do not panic! Once you have identified the tightest side, the one that will alert you to a feeling of discomfort, you can work to reduce it! This posture is ideal for developing balance and stability and will help you find harmony in your hips.

Upper body stimulation with raised arms contributes to maximum use of the diaphragm muscles. Breathing is thus more pronounced with open shoulders and arms. This asana strengthens the shoulders and chest and thus corrects bad postures.

The body is an energy sponge and it has a memory. Want to reduce stress? It accumulates in the hips and psoas.

By practicing this posture, you accentuate the opening of the hips, the strengthening of the glutes and finally the engagement of the psoas muscles which greatly help to reduce stress. The longer you hold in the pose, the more stress you eliminate!

Inhale, spread your feet apart (well more than hip distance) and bend your knees. You arrive at a half-squat posture.

Your knees are in one line as are your heels. Your toes are looking outward. Legs perpendicular to the ground. Retrovert the pelvis, tuck in the navel so that the coccyx looks at the ground.

Open your arms parallel to the floor on each side. Keep them in line with your shoulders without ever lowering them. Face your palms outward and bend your elbows so that your arms form a 90-degree angle. You now have your arms perpendicular to the ground, a so-called "cactus" position.

Once your legs are engaged and your feet are firmly planted on the ground, keep your knees bent. Sit more and more in the posture without straining on the descent. Bring your tailbone closer to the ground while your upper body remains straight and stable.

Look ahead, open your heart! Bring the shoulders back, bring the shoulder blades together and lengthen the spine to the top of the head.

Well done! You have just achieved the posture of the Goddess. An inner power frees you from your emotional blockages and gives you confidence like a goddess!

I like to add arm movements to this pose. You can inhale raise your arms to the sky, clenched fists, and exhale release your arms downward, opening your hands and letting out a bold, liberating RRRHHHHAAA.

HALF SALAMANDER AND FULL SALAMANDER

THE HALF SALAMANDER

This is called the half salamander because your eyes move while your head remains still, similar to the behavior of a salamander.

The half salamander practice is used to stimulate and release the vagus nerve. It provides more mobility to the thoracic spine, opening movement in the joints between the ribs and sternum, thereby increasing respiratory capacity, which helps reduce anxiety and stress. It also reduces forward head posture by aligning the head with the rest of the spine, much like a salamander that has no neck.

Sit or stand in a comfortable position with your head facing forward.

Shift your gaze to the right without turning your head.

Tilt your head toward your right shoulder and hold the position for 30 to 60 seconds.

Let your head return to its neutral position and move your eyes to look forward again.

Repeat the same steps on the other side.

Half salamander stimulates the vagus nerves – the system that controls your heart rate – and triggers a relaxation response in our body.

THE FULL SALAMANDER

This one is harder to do if you're in the office, so it's a great exercise to try at home.

Kneel on all fours with your head facing down.

Look to the left without turning your head.

Tilt your head to the left.

Allow your left spine to twist with your head tilted to the left.

Hold for 30 to 60 seconds

Bring your head and spine to center to straighten up.

Repeat the same steps on the other side.

Ideally you should hold the position until you yawn, which will be a sign that your nervous system has released the pressure.

ROCKING STARFISH

Here is the only time in your life when you will be advised to do the Starfish ;-)

Lay flat on your back, on your bed, or on the floor with your arms and legs extended like a starfish.

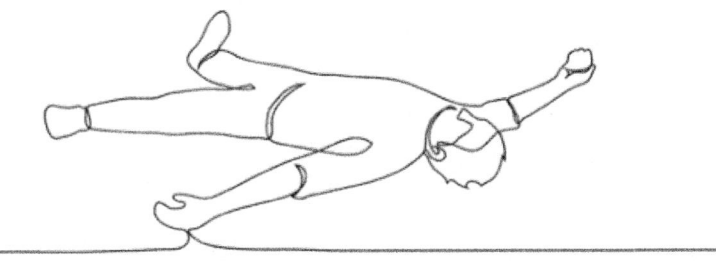

From there, you will just move your feet, you just point and flex your feet, so that you initiate a tiny rocking move of your whole body.

It's not a big move at all, you just rock very gently back and forth.

When you do this move for 2 to 5 minutes, keep breathing very deeply and soundly.

It's a very relaxing move, you may want to release tension while crying also there. Feel free to do it!

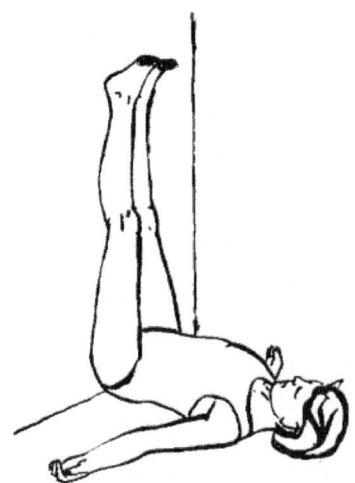

It's a fun, relaxing and beneficial posture that we can all benefit from.

Because of its calming benefits, this pose is often practiced before bed.

It relaxes and calms the mind, it promotes better sleep.

It's easy, it's fun and the whole family can do it together.

Additionally, posture also helps promote balance and well-being in all systems of the entire body, including:

❧ Strengthens the immune system

❧ Balances the hormonal system

❧ Calms the nervous system

❧ Stabilizes the digestive and elimination systems

❧ Regulates the respiratory system

Make it a family tradition before bed and notice the changes this simple posture can bring to the whole family.

This pose is usually done by resting your legs against a wall, but can also be done without using a wall for support.

Ideally you can practice it on your bed, that way you are ready to go on to a good night's sleep!

Start by lying on your back. You might like to grab a pillow to place under your lower back or under your head, maybe both.

Raise your legs toward the ceiling. If you are against a wall, gently place your legs against the wall. Slide your butt as close to the wall as possible, you want to make sure you don't lift your hips.

Place your arms on the floor next to your body. Palms facing up, breathe deeply into your stomach.

Hold this posture for as long as you are comfortable, or until your legs tingle.

Listen to music or take the opportunity to do deep breathing exercises or meditate.

When you're ready, roll onto your side and rest there for a few minutes.

Slowly and gently, return to a sitting position.

By regularly incorporating legs up the wall into your life, it can be an easy way to relax.

Then you'll be ready for a good night's sleep!

ZZZZZZZZZzzzzzzzzzzzzz

SHADOW BOXING

There are many mindfulness techniques we hear about that positively influence our well-being and reduce our stress, but have you ever thought that boxing could be one of them? Interestingly enough, boxing is a great technique to relieve some stress, whether it's eliminating that anxiety or getting rid of pent-up anger. This is an unusual mechanism, but one that has great advantages.

To begin with, boxing is defined as a physical activity and sport that involves fighting an opponent with the fists, using fighting gloves. It seems ironic how beneficial it is for your mental health to punch someone, but boxing can be done alone at home.

Any form of exercise releases endorphins – Endorphins are a type of endogenous opioid, but they are formed in our bodies, unlike opiates like morphine or heroin. They are basically hormones that play a role in reducing pain, regulating the heart and blood vessels, breathing and much more. So, in simplistic terms, these hormones are released to induce a calming effect, and here we can understand how good one feels after exercise.

Boxing is a form of anger management and stress relief. Imagine being able to release all your pent-up anger with just one punch. Managing your emotions is a difficult thing to do, and you need to do it the right way – by hitting things, not people...! It also relieves any pent-up stress you may be feeling.

By channeling your focus on the present and avoiding negative thoughts and worries, boxing can help relieve symptoms of anxiety and depression.

Invisible boxing is a great way to release stress and tension.

It can also help increase energy levels, improve coordination and balance, and build self-confidence. Additionally, invisible boxing can help strengthen the muscles of the arms, shoulders and chest.

Concretely, it's very simple and you don't need any equipment.

You can put movie images like that of Rocky in your head, imagine your worst enemy and your biggest problem in front of you and throw your fists forward alternately.

Blow off steam until you feel ready to stop.

If it helps, you can also hit a pillow for example.

Shadow boxing is based on the principle of relaxation without intention of harm. This is done for a short duration to reduce physical effort and create a feeling of tranquility. Shadow boxing is a form of meditation, allowing you to feel at peace and escape the distractions of daily life. The idea is that this state also carries over to our daily activities so that we can remain calm in stressful situations.

BREATHING TECHNIQUES

There are many, but ultimately we can remember mainly 7, which have proven their effectiveness in managing stress and anxiety.

Breathing is an automatic function of the body controlled by the respiratory center of the brain. When we feel stressed, our breathing rhythm and pattern changes as part of the "fight or flight response."

Fortunately, we also have the power to deliberately change our own breathing. Scientific studies have shown that controlling your breathing can help manage stress. Many people use their breathing to promote relaxation and reduce stress.

The main role of respiration is to absorb oxygen and expel carbon dioxide through the movement of the lungs. The muscles that control the movement of the lungs are the diaphragm (a layer of muscle beneath the lungs) and the muscles between the ribs.

When a person is stressed, their breathing pattern changes. Typically, an anxious person takes short, shallow breaths, using their shoulders rather than their diaphragm to move air in and out of their lungs. This style of breathing disrupts the balance of gases in the body.

Excessive, shallow breathing, or hyperventilation, can prolong feelings of anxiety by worsening the physical symptoms of stress. Controlling your breathing can help improve some of these symptoms.

When a person is relaxed, they breathe through their nose slowly, evenly, and gently. Deliberately copying a relaxed breathing pattern appears to calm the nervous system that controls the body's involuntary functions.

Controlled breathing can cause physiological changes such as:

- decrease in blood pressure and heart rate

- reduced levels of stress hormones in the blood

- reduction of lactic acid accumulation in muscle tissues

- balanced levels of oxygen and carbon dioxide in the blood

- improved functioning of the immune system

- increased physical energy

- increased feelings of calm and well-being.

There are different breathing techniques to induce relaxation. Essentially, the overall goal is to move from upper thoracic breathing to abdominal breathing. You will need a quiet, relaxed environment where you will not be disturbed for 10 to 20 minutes. Set an alarm if you don't want to lose track of time.

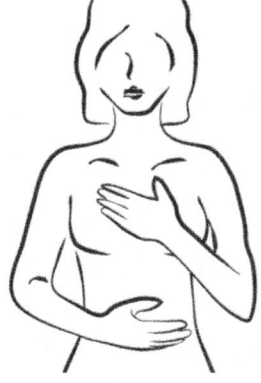

4-7-8

4-7-8 breathing can help you regain control of your breathing. This involves inhaling for 4 seconds, holding your breath for 7 seconds and exhaling for 8 seconds.

Based on an ancient yogic method called pranayama, the technique was developed by Dr. Andrew Weil. When practiced regularly, this technique may help some people fall asleep more quickly.

Breathing techniques aim to bring the body into a state of deep relaxation. Specific patterns that involve holding the breath for a period of time allow your body to replenish its oxygen. Techniques like 4-7-8 can give your organs and tissues a much-needed oxygen boost.

Relaxation practices also help restore balance to the body and regulate the fight or flight response we feel when we are stressed. This is especially helpful if you suffer from insomnia due to anxiety or worries about what happened today or what might happen tomorrow. Swirling thoughts and concerns can prevent us from getting good rest.

The 4-7-8 technique forces the mind and body to focus on regulating breathing, rather than replaying your worries when you lie down at night. Practitioners claim it can soothe a racing heart or calm exhausted nerves. Dr. Weil even described it as a "natural tranquilizer for the nervous system."

People with mild sleep disorders, anxiety, and stress may find 4-7-8 breathing helpful in overcoming distraction and slipping into a relaxed state.

Over time and with repeated practice, practitioners of 4-7-8 breathing say it becomes more and more powerful. It is said that at first its effects are not as apparent. You might feel a little dizzy the first time you try it. Practicing 4-7-8 breathing at least twice a day might provide better results for some people than those who only practice it once.

To practice 4-7-8 breathing, find a place to sit or lie down comfortably. Make sure you maintain good posture, especially at the beginning. If you are using this technique to fall asleep, it is best to lie down.

Prepare for the practice by resting the tip of your tongue against the roof of your mouth, just behind your upper front teeth. You will need to keep your tongue in place throughout the practice. It takes practice not to move your tongue when you exhale. Exhaling during the 4-7-8 breath may be easier for some people when they purse their lips.

The following steps should all be performed in the one-breath cycle:

First, let your lips open. Make a whistling noise,

Exhale completely through your mouth.

Next, close your lips, inhaling silently through your nose as you count to four in your head.

Then, for seven seconds, hold your breath.

Make another whistling exhale from your mouth for eight seconds.

When you breathe in again, you initiate a new breathing cycle. Practice this pattern for four to eight full breaths.

The held breath (for seven seconds) is the most critical part of this practice. It is also recommended to only practice 4-7-8 breathing for four breaths when you are starting out. You can gradually work your way up to eight full breaths.

This breathing technique should not be practiced in an environment where you are not ready to completely relax. Although it does not necessarily have to be used to fall asleep, it can still put the practitioner into a state of deep relaxation. Make sure you don't need to be fully alert immediately after practicing your breathing cycles.

RESONANT BREATHING

Cardiac coherence or resonant breathing is an effective method accessible to everyone, which has no contraindications. But you have to practice it regularly to reap all its benefits.

Cardiac coherence can be defined as a state of balance between the sympathetic nervous system and the parasympathetic nervous system. The first is the adaptation system which is triggered in the event of threat, the second is the recovery system, once the danger has passed.

Breathing in cardiac coherence is not natural. In general, we breathe 12 to 15 times per minute while resting. Heart rate is not constant, it varies constantly. It is cardiac chaos which is the normal state of the heart rate, and proof that we manage to adapt quickly to different situations in our environment. Cardiac coherence is not spontaneous breathing. In cardiac coherence, we breathe 6 times in a row per minute, voluntarily and regularly.

Each time we inhale, the heart speeds up because we stimulate the sympathetic system, and each time we exhale, the heart slows down because we stimulate the parasympathetic system.

The first advantage of cardiac coherence is its beneficial effect in combating stress. Its regular practice helps reduce the level of cortisol, the stress hormone, and increase DHEA, the hormone of youth, which antagonizes cortisol. Ultimately, we limit the risk of fatigue and exhaustion, we find it easier to let go and gain distance from events. We reduce anxiety and the risk of depression.

Its principle is simple: cardiac coherence consists of taking six breaths per minute for five minutes and three times a day. In detail, this amounts to inhaling for 5 seconds then exhaling for 5 seconds and this 6 times in a row.

At first, for some people, this may seem complicated. We can therefore start by inhaling for 3 seconds and exhaling for 3 seconds, then inhaling for 4 seconds and exhaling for 4 seconds, but the result is less convincing. The important thing is, above all, to equalize the two times: inspiration and expiration.

Breathing in cardiac coherence immediately provides a soothing effect, a feeling of calm, serenity, well-being. But these benefits are fleeting, they last between 3 and 6 hours after the end of the exercise, and on average 4 hours. To benefit from it in the long term, there is only one solution: practice cardiac coherence three times a day, every day!

The first session takes place in the morning.

This is the most important. It should be practiced as soon as possible after getting up because at this time of the day, the secretion of cortisol, the stress hormone, is greatest. Exercising cardiac coherence will therefore reduce it if it is high, which is the case in stressed people.

The second session before lunch time.

That's about 4 hours after the first one. The second session allows you to refocus and alleviate the events that occurred in the morning. It also prepares for good digestion, it limits the risk of drowsiness after meals and ensures good mental clarity to work all afternoon.

The third session at the end of the afternoon.

When the rhythm of life will change, especially with the end of the work day and the return home. It will ensure a relaxed evening, and a better night.

We choose a quiet, comfortable place where no one will disturb us during the session. To ritualize the practice of cardiac coherence, you can always choose the same place, as far as possible.

We put ourselves in a sitting position or, possibly, standing, but not lying down;

Sit with your back straight, with just your lower back resting on the backrest. Stretch your spine as much as possible, and place your feet on the ground and your hands on your thighs. Avoid crossing your legs so as not to compress your abdomen.

Before starting the cardiac coherence exercise, empty your lungs and stomach. And then we can begin. We inhale through the stomach, inflating it, and exhale gently through the mouth, deflating the stomach.

So, we don't wait any longer, we get started!

UJJAYI BREATHING OR OCEANIC BREATHING

Ujjayi is also known as ocean breathing or victorious breathing. Ujjayi is composed of two words: "ud" which means a feeling of superiority or power, and "jaya" means victory, conquest or success, which gives it the meaning of victorious breathing. It is called ocean breathing because of the ocean wave-like sound when exhaling and inhaling. The sound is produced by the friction of the throat with air.

Ujjayi is both a fun and effective form of breathing for anxiety (and also mental focus). It only takes a little practice to learn it, so read on!

Ujjayi Breath is also called Darth Vader breathing (for all you Star Wars fans) because your breathing will sound like ocean waves or Darth Vader. This sound comes from the constriction in the back of your throat (which we'll practice below).

Let's try:

Start in a comfortable seated position, sitting up straight.

Contract the back of your throat

Inhale through your nose while maintaining this constriction

Pretend you are fogging up a mirror while exhaling through your mouth.

Inhale through your nose again while maintaining this constriction

This time, close your lips and exhale through your nose (still pretending to fog up the mirror)

Continue this inhaling and exhaling through your nose for 10 cycles or as long as you like.

DOUBLE INHALE AND SIGH

The physiological sigh or cyclic sigh is simple, can be done anywhere, and (bonus) costs nothing. If you feel tense, take two sharp inhales, usually through your nose, followed by a prolonged exhale through your mouth. After just one or two of these sighing exercises, you may feel more relaxed, but to get the full effect, it is recommended to repeat the cyclical sighs for about five minutes. The second inhale of the double inhale is really important, because it not only allows more oxygen to be taken in, but also carbon dioxide to be released.

And exhaling is also essential, as it activates the parasympathetic nervous system which then slows your heart rate and has an overall calming effect on the body.

Instead of waiting for your breathing cycle to unconsciously reset while you're stressed, neuroscientist Dr. Andrew Huberman and his colleagues at Stanford University have developed a breathing technique that helps you calm down and relax as quickly as possible, using reflex sighs.

Simply:

Inhale long, through your nose, until it is almost full then inhale again quickly, until it is full (the double inhale) before exhaling long and slowly through your mouth.

Repeating this 2 or 3 times will bring you back to a more relaxed state and help you regain a sense of control and stability in the circumstances. Ideally practice 5 minutes several times a day.

You have small air bags in your lungs, which increase the volume of air you can breathe in. These sacs collapse over time and as a result oxygen levels begin to drop and carbon dioxide levels rise in the blood and body, and this is a large part of the signaling response to stress.

The double inhale of the physiological sigh "pops" the air sacs (called alveoli) open, allowing oxygen to enter and allowing you to discharge the carbon dioxide in the long exhaled sigh.

It is a real-time tool that can be deployed anytime, anywhere to reduce stress.

One important thing to point out is that your heart rate will always take a little longer to slow down than your breathing rate. This is because the neural circuits controlling the heart operate at a slower rate than those in the lungs, so you'll need to be a little patient with your heart each time you do this!

VOOOO SOUND

I'm a fan of Peter Levine's work and came across his "Vooo breathing" exercise in one of his books.

It's quite fascinating and at the same time very simple.

The idea is to breathe deeply through the belly, focus our attention on our breathing and, in a deep foghorn voice, we exhale with the word "voooooo". It seems a little strange at first, but I promise it's an effective way to induce a feeling of calm. This can be extremely helpful for trauma survivors who struggle to feel relaxed and calm; especially after reminders of their trauma. So why does this "voo breathing" work?

Breathing is one of the most fascinating trauma recovery resources we have at the tip of our tongue...literally!

When we slowly breathe in through our nose and out through our mouth, we stimulate both the sympathetic (fight and flight) and parasympathetic (rest and digest) nervous systems.

So breathing can give your brain and body a much-needed break.

So boom! Inhaling and exhaling while stimulating the vagus nerve creates a beautiful recipe for feelings of calm.

Start by sitting down.

Find a place to sit and rest. Place your feet on the floor and rest comfortably in your chair. Close your eyes if you feel safe, or if you choose to keep your eyes open, keep a low, steady gaze.

Become aware of your breathing.

Begin to calm your breathing. Simply note each breathing cycle as it enters and exits. Just notice. Would not change a thing.

Inhale deeply.

Now start allowing yourself to take a deep, slow breath in through your nose and fill your belly with air. Side note: make sure you are breathing into your stomach and not your chest. You'll know you're breathing from your stomach if you inhale and your shoulders don't continue to rise and fall as you breathe.

Exhale with "VOO".

As you exhale, allow yourself to make a deep foghorn sound with the word "voo," for three counts (or as long as you can exhale comfortably, the longer the better). Let the sound vibrate and resonate in your chest, arms and even legs. Feel and enjoy the deep vibrations of the "voo" sound.

Repeat the breathing cycles.

Continue the cycles for 3 to 5 minutes or as long as you enjoy the activity. We know that 3-5 minutes of breathing can really change your blood oxygen levels and start to stimulate positive changes in your neurochemistry!

Bring your focus back to the room.

Begin to become aware of your body, perhaps by turning your wrists or ankles. When you are ready, open your eyes and return to the room.

Just as we learn to swim when we are calm and not drowning, it is important to learn new coping skills when we are calm and not panicking.

ALTERNATE BREATHING RIGHT/LEFT NOSTRIL

Nadi Shodhana Pranayama, also called alternate-nostril breathing, is a breathing exercise alternating between the nostrils. This technique helps balance both sides of the brain, reduce stress and anxiety, and improve digestion.

As useful for starting the day off on the right foot as for getting to sleep more easily, alternate breathing is an easy practice to access, provided you don't have a cold. Ideally, it is practiced seated, legs crossed, back straight and left hand placed on the left knee. Elevating yourself by sitting on a cushion can make posture easier.

With your eyes closed, begin by inhaling through both nostrils. Index and middle fingers folded, close your right nostril with your thumb and exhale through the left nostril. Then inhale to the left for a count of 4, right nostril still blocked. Close the left nostril with your ring finger and then exhale through the right nostril for a count of 8. Inhale to the right, left nostril still blocked, for a count of 4. Exhale to the left, this time blocking the right nostril. Continue like this for at least 5 minutes.

The thumb blocks the right nostril and the little and ring fingers block the left nostril. Close the right nostril with your thumb and inhale through the left nostril for 4 seconds. Close both nostrils and hold your breath for 4 seconds. Unblock the right nostril and exhale for 4 seconds.

If the pace indicated is not suitable, everyone can adapt it to their own feelings. However, making sure that the exhalation always lasts longer than the inspiration.

To increase the effects of this rebalancing breathing, it is possible to add air retention phases. After inhaling for 4 seconds, hold your breath for 4 seconds then exhale for 8 seconds. If this air retention phase does not cause any dizziness or unpleasant sensations, you can very gradually extend the duration of the apnea to 8, 12 then 16 seconds. But be careful, this is not a competition, do not try to exceed your own limits.

LION'S BREATH

Practicing Lion's Breath regularly helps relieve stress and tension.

Lion's breath, or Simhasana in Sanskrit, is another breathing practice. You can do this alone or as part of a longer practice. Sticking out your tongue and roaring like a lion might be just what you need to relax or express yourself.

You can use lion's breath to help clear your throat if you have a dry mouth or a ticklish throat. It also promotes relaxation of the facial and neck muscles. This is useful when you have used these muscles for speaking or concentrating.

And of course, this exercises your lungs with special attention.

Lion's breath stimulates your vocal cords and diaphragm. This has made it a popular breathing exercise for singers and people with speech disorders, such as stuttering.

And because you have to put self-awareness aside to practice it, lion's breath can help you in other aspects of life, like when you want to express yourself in certain situations but find yourself running away.

.

You may also find that lion's breath helps you release your emotions or thoughts.

This is especially good to do in the morning to energize yourself or after an intense workout to blow away the heat.

You can practice Lion Breathing in a variety of positions, including sitting cross-legged on the floor, sitting in a chair, or in Lion Pose (see above). Choose the one that suits you best. You can also sit on a block or cushion.

Whatever sitting position you have chosen, press your hands firmly on your knees or on the floor and spread your fingers as wide as possible like the lion's claws.

Inhale deeply through your nose.

Open your mouth wide, stick your tongue out and extend it as far toward your chin as possible, then exhale forcefully through your mouth.

As you exhale, make a "ha" sound and try to bring your drishti (focused gaze) towards your third eye (the space between your eyebrows) or the tip of your nose, opening your eyes wide, squinting a little while fat.

Repeat 4 to 6 times. If you have your feet/legs crossed, change the crossing of your legs halfway through your reps.

Finally, breathe deeply and normally for a few moments.

MEDITATIONS

LOVING KINDNESS MEDITATION

This meditation invites us to cultivate the seeds of kindness already present in us and to make them grow to develop openness and kindness in our heart.

We thus develop our ability to live more and more in harmony with ourselves, with others and to put the nature of human beings into perspective, to find the best in each of them.

A kindness that is addressed to oneself, to those close to us, to our more distant daily circle (shopkeepers, friends, etc.) and finally to people with whom we have no affection.

This last step may seem delicate and difficult, which is why it is important to do it gradually.

It's about bringing happiness to yourself by meditating but also to others by perceiving the connection that connects us all.

So let's begin this simple kindness meditation: offering good wishes and compassion to others and to yourself.

Find a comfortable sitting position. You can even place your hand on your heart. Let your eyes close or lower your gaze to the floor.

Start by visualizing yourself, and sending yourself compassion and kindness, wish yourself to be happy, healthy, free from suffering etc...Find the words that seem right to you, imagine you as your own best friend.

Then think about someone you really respect and admire, and who really loves you in return.

Notice how you feel when you think about this person.

Make a nice wish and send it to him.

What would make him/her happy? "May she be healthy" for example

Then, think of someone else you love and care about: a family member, a friend, etc. Just think of that person, sending them a nice wish.

We're going to move on to a more neutral person. Maybe someone you don't know very well: a relative you see occasionally, someone who delivers your mail. Just think about that person and imagine yourself sending them some kind of pleasant wish.

Finally, think about someone who has frustrated you lately, someone who is a little difficult. Send that last person a kind wish: something nice for them in their life.

We can extend this meditation to all living beings on this Earth, but you do not have to go that far at first. Then stay in this position for a few breaths, trying to feel kindness and gratitude for those around you and for yourself.

BODY SCAN MEDITATION

Begin by making yourself comfortable. Sit in a chair and allow your back to be straight, but not stiff, with your feet on the ground. You could also do this practice standing or if you prefer, you can lie down and have your head supported.

Your hands could be resting gently in your lap or at your side. Allow your eyes to close, or to remain open with a soft gaze.

Take several long, slow, deep breaths. Breathing in fully and exhaling slowly. Breathe in through your nose and out through your nose or mouth. Feel your stomach expand on an inhale and relax and let go as you exhale. Begin to let go of noises around you.

Begin to shift your attention from outside to inside yourself. If you are distracted by sounds in the room, simply notice this and bring your focus back to your breathing. Now slowly bring your attention down to your feet. Begin observing sensations in your feet.

You might want to wiggle your toes a little, feeling your toes against your socks or shoes. Just notice, without judgment. You might imagine sending your breath down to your feet, as if the breath is traveling through the nose to the lungs and through the abdomen all the way down to your feet. And then back up again out through your nose and lungs.

Perhaps you don't feel anything at all. That is fine, too. Just allow yourself to feel the sensation of not feeling anything.

When you are ready, allow your feet to dissolve in your mind's eye and move your attention up to your ankles, calves, knees and thighs.

Observe the sensations you are experiencing throughout your legs. Breathe into and breathe out of the legs. If your mind begins to wander during this exercise, gently notice this without judgment and bring your mind back to noticing the sensations in your legs. If you notice any discomfort, pain or stiffness, don't judge this.

Just simply notice it. Observe how all sensations rise and fall, shift and change moment to moment. Notice how no sensation is permanent. Just observe and allow the sensations to be in the moment, just as they are. Breathe into and out from the legs. Then on the next out breath, allow the legs to dissolve in your mind.

And move to the sensations in your lower back and pelvis. Softening and releasing as you breathe in and out. Slowly move your attention up to your mid back and upper back. Become curious about the sensations here. You may become aware of sensations in the muscle, temperature or points of contact with furniture or the bed.

With each outbreath, you may let go of tension you are carrying. And then very gently shift your focus to your stomach and all the internal organs here. Perhaps you notice the feeling of clothing, the process of digestion or the belly rising or falling with each breath.

If you notice opinions arising about these areas, gently let these go and return to noticing sensations. As you continue to breathe, bring your awareness to the chest and heart region and just notice your heartbeat. Observe how the chest rises during the inhale and how the chest falls during the exhale. Let go of any judgments that may arise.

On the next outbreath, shift the focus to your hands and fingertips. See if you can channel your breathing into and out of this area as if you are breathing into and out from your hands. If your mind wanders, gently bring it back to the sensations in your hands.

And then, on the next outbreath, shift the focus and bring your awareness up into your arms.

Observe the sensations or lack of sensations that may be occurring there. You might notice some difference between the left arm and the right arm – no need to judge this. As you exhale, you may experience the arm soften and release tensions.

Continue to breathe and shift focus to the neck, shoulder and throat region. This is an area where we often have tension. Be with the sensations here. It could be tightness, rigidity or holding. You may notice the shoulders moving along with the breath.

Let go of any thoughts or stories you are telling about this area. As you breathe, you may feel tension rolling off your shoulders. On the next outbreath, shift your focus and direct your attention to the scalp, head and face. Observe all of the sensations occurring there.

Notice the movement of the air as you breathe into or out of the nostrils or mouth. As you exhale, you might notice the softening of any tension you may be holding. And now, let your attention to expand out to include the entire body as a whole.

Bring into your awareness the top of your head down to the bottom of your toes. Feel the gentle rhythm of the breath as it moves through the body.

As you come to the end of this practice, take a full, deep breath, taking in all the energy of this practice. Exhale fully. And when you are ready, open your eyes and return your attention to the present moment.

As you become fully alert and awake, consider setting the intention that this practice of building awareness will benefit everyone you come in contact with today

MINDFULNESS MEDITATION

Mindfulness is about being fully in the present moment, noticing our thoughts, feelings, and experiences without judgment.

This could be what you feel, hear, or anything else you notice. There is no particular state of calm that you need to achieve and it is not about emptying your mind, it is simply about an honest and caring look at what you are experiencing at the moment. We observe our thoughts as if they were clouds in the sky.

First, make yourself comfortable in a chair or on the floor. Sit up straight with your feet flat on the floor, your arms and legs uncrossed and your hands resting on your knees. Let your eyes close or focus on a point in front of you.

Inhale and exhale gently.

Notice the sensation of your own breath as you inhale and exhale.

Now try to imagine that you are lying on a grassy hill on a warm spring day. Imagine feeling the ground beneath you, the smell of grass, and the sound of nearby trees being blown by the wind.

Now imagine that you are looking up at the sky and watching the clouds pass by.

Begin to become aware of your thoughts and feelings. Every time a thought comes to mind, imagine placing it on one of these clouds and allowing it to float.

If you think in words or images, put them on a cloud and let them pass.

The goal is to continue to observe the sky and let the clouds pass.

Try not to change what appears on the clouds one way or another. If the clouds disappear or you mentally go elsewhere, stop and notice what is happening, and slowly return to looking at the clouds in the sky.

If you have any ideas or feelings about this exercise, place them on clouds as well. If the thoughts stop, just look at the sky and the clouds. Sooner or later, your thoughts should start again.

You simply observe each thought or feeling like a word or picture on a cloud. It is normal and natural to lose track of this exercise, and this will continue. When you notice you're losing track, just go back to looking at the clouds in the sky.

Let the clouds float at their own pace and place any thought, feeling, sensation or image that comes to mind on a cloud and let it float away.

Finally, bring your attention back to your breathing. Notice again the steady rhythm of your breathing that is with you all the time. Then bring your awareness back to the sitting position. Slowly open your eyes and notice what you can see. Push your feet onto the floor and stretch.

Happy to see you again! So how was it?

The objective of this exercise is not to no longer have thoughts, or to be ultra calm, it is to understand the principle of "defusion" with one's thoughts.

If we can observe our thoughts, that means we are NOT our thoughts.

And by realizing this, we can distance ourselves more from them, and be less influenced by what they tell us. It's a first step towards inner peace!

OTHER TOOLS:

Apart from postures, movements and breathing exercises, there are also other practices and lifestyle changes that can have a real impact on your mind and well-being.

We will see some of them in the following pages.

EARTHING OR GROUNDING

Earthing, or grounding the body, is a simple, powerful, and easy-to-practice way to reduce stress and thus strengthen your well-being and health.

Earthing generates a shift of the nervous system from the sympathetic (fight or flight mode associated with stress) to the calming and relaxing parasympathetic mode.

Earthing has a normalizing effect on cortisol, the stress hormone.

Earthing promotes better sleep and reduces inflammation and pain.

What we seek to do using this practice is to connect to the energy of the Earth. Its weak electrical energy passes through our body and unites us with it. In doing so, we live entirely in the present moment to fully appreciate this bond that is being created. Several other benefits are also listed, but the advantage of grounding is above all the fact of anchoring yourself in the present.

The best place to practice grounding is therefore outdoors, where contact with the earth is more direct, but it is also possible to do it indoors.

WALKING BARE FOOT

Both inside and out. When walking barefoot, the connection to the earth is very direct. You can feel the heat, the cold, the different textures and it is very relaxing, as long as you do it in full awareness, that is to say paying full attention to the effect of the floor on the surface of his feet.

« TREE HUGGING »

We can easily find trees close to us. A tree several hundred years old is even better.

A large, strong one with an impressive diameter. We can go give him a hug occasionally. We feel the pressure of our trunk on our sternum, in the heart chakra area.

It has an extremely calming effect. In spring, summer and fall, we can lean against a tree to write, read and try to feel a very strong connection and the energy that flows through it when we take the time to concentrate.

Indeed, we can be afraid of ridicule. From the incomprehension of other walkers in the forest. But forget about others, think about yourself and all the benefits that this simple gesture can bring you.

No special technique is necessary! You just have to choose your tree, a big one, no matter the species. This tree must "speak" to you.

Hug him, rest one cheek on his trunk, close your eyes, breathe deeply and regularly, clear your mind. Give free rein to your emotions.

Feel the strength and energy that emanates from it. Listen to him live.

Feel its vibrations, its noises, its creaks, and its life.

A few minutes of cuddling are enough to feel good or better!

NATURE OR FOREST BATHING

Another way to perceive the environment in all its smells is by going for a walk. Whether in the forest, by the water or in a flower garden, taking the time to soak up the smells has a fantastic effect on our connection to the earth.

BATH AND WATER

All water sources are filled with beautiful energy. Rivers, lakes, waterfalls, the ocean. Water that stirs, water that carries, water that soothes.

If it's not easy to have access to one of these water sources in your surroundings, bathing is the closest thing to water in nature.

The pressure that the water exerts on the body adds something even more magical to this way of getting grounded.

STONES

Their weight, their freshness, their colors, they emanate something beautiful. Depending on the mood, depending on the energy level, we are attracted to different stones.

You can use a palm stone in particular, or a pebble that can be found at the sea.

Very smooth and rounded, which can be held in the hand to calm down. By touching it, we already feel a connection.

Technically, by taking an object, whatever it may be, you can also ground yourself. It's about taking the time to really feel the object in your hand. In full awareness, feel it, feel it, weigh it, take the time to fully absorb its color, its smell, its texture, its heat, etc...

COLD WATER THERAPY

COLD SHOWER

We know that repeated exposure to cold water significantly reduces the body's defensive response. The key is to stay in the water long enough to acclimatize, slowly building up your body's responses. Avoid getting to the point where you start shivering, get out just before that happens. Learn to control your breathing so you don't hyperventilate.

Taking deep breaths and relaxing the body before entering the water (whether in the shower or in the sea) will begin to send signals to your body that you are relaxed and that what is about to going without is OK. (Remember to research and prepare in advance and if you have underlying health conditions, seek medical attention).

As you repeat your cold water exposures, your body prolongs the need to trigger your fight, flight, and freeze response (sympathetic nervous response) and this approach is then introduced into your daily life. You will begin to notice that your response to normal stress (being late, no phone signal, or screaming children) also improves.

This is precisely how meditation works. You train your mind and body to learn that not every stress you encounter during your day requires extreme responses. It can reduce anxiety, stress and improve the mood of people suffering from depression.

If your mind is racing and you're overwhelmed, take a dip in cold water and then you'll just focus on your breathing and what's happening at that moment.

Cold showers are difficult at first, but they can greatly improve the function of our vagus nerve. How? Because when you take a cold shower, the first shock of the cold water (better to start with the water on your back first), will make you inhale briefly and sharply, and you will have an initial reaction of wanting to stop.

Get out of there or tense your muscles. By deliberately exhaling long and slow and relaxing your muscles, you will begin to adapt to the cold.

When this happens, the sympathetic nervous system slows down and the parasympathetic system takes over, directly affecting the vagus nerve.

It is important to maintain regular breathing when exposed to cold water to keep the parasympathetic system functioning. This is difficult to do, but with practice you will notice that other neurochemicals will also be released, such as endorphins, which will have a lasting positive impact. You don't have to take a cold shower for very long. Thirty seconds to a minute of cold shower is more than enough. It might also be a good idea to leave the last 30 seconds to 1 minute of your regular shower to get used to the cold water temperature.

SIP ON ICE COLD WATER

Research published in Scientific Reports has found that drinking plenty of water combats dehydration which can cause weakening of the vagus nerve. But for an added bonus, opt for cold water.

Vagus nerve activity increased by 39% in people who drank a glass of ice water while it decreased by 5% in those who drank room temperature water.

Experts explain that cold water acts on the nerve endings in the esophagus, causing them to send stimulating signals to the vagus.

COLD WATER ON THE FACE

Triggering a response known as the diving reflex stimulates the function of the vagus nerve. And it doesn't require diving into a cold pool. Instead, just take a cold compress.

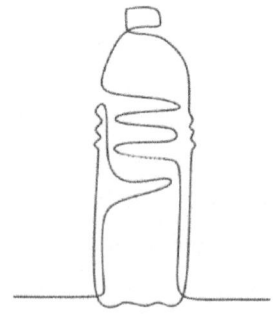

In a Buffalo University study, measurements of vagus nerve activity increased by up to 163% in people who had a cooled face. The tip: apply ice water to your cheeks, forehead and closed eyes for three minutes.

Simply fill a zip bag with ice water and place it on the upper half of your face. Or immerse your face in a bowl of ice water.

It seems pretty extreme but really effective for panic attack!

MUSIC

Music can have a profound effect on both the emotions and the body. Faster music can make you feel more alert and concentrate better. Upbeat music can make you more optimistic and positive about life. A slower pace can calm your mind and relax your muscles, soothing you while releasing the stress of the day. Music is effective for relaxation and stress management.

Research supports these personal experiences with music. Current findings indicate that music at around 60 beats per minute can cause the brain to synchronize with the rhythm, causing alpha brain waves (frequencies of 8 to 14 hertz, or cycles per second).

This alpha brain wave is present when we are relaxed. To induce sleep (a 5 hertz delta brain wave), a person may need to spend at least 45 minutes, in a relaxed position, listening to calming music. Researchers at Stanford University say listening to music appears to be able to change brain function to the same extent as medications. They noted that music is something that almost everyone can access and makes it a simple stress-reducing tool.

So, what type of music best reduces stress? What's a little surprising is that Native American, Celtic, and Indian stringed instruments, drums, and flutes are very effective at relaxing the mind, even when played moderately loud. The sounds of rain, thunder, and nature sounds can also be relaxing, especially when mixed with other music, such as light jazz, classical (the "largo" movement), and music easy to listen to.

Since in music we are rarely told the beats per minute, how do you choose the relaxation music that suits you best? The answer is partly up to you: first you have to like the music being played, then it has to relax you. You can start by simply exploring music on the internet. Some may relax you, others may not. Forcing yourself to listen to relaxing music that irritates you can create tension, not reduce it. If this happens, try looking for alternatives. It's important to remember that calming your mind doesn't automatically mean you'll feel sleepy. This means that your brain and body are relaxed and with your new state of calm, you can then function at your best in many activities.

FOREST BATHING

Whether you call it a new age trend or a mindfulness practice (or a little of both), what exactly is forest bathing?

The term emerged in Japan in the 1980s as a physiological and psychological exercise called shinrin-yoku ("forest bathing" or "soaking up the atmosphere of the forest"). The objective was twofold: to offer an antidote to professional burnout due to the technological boom and to encourage residents to reconnect with and protect the country's forests.

The Japanese quickly adopted this form of ecotherapy. In the 1990s, researchers began studying the physiological benefits of forest bathing, providing scientific data supporting what we innately know: time spent immersed in nature is good for us. While the term shinrin-yoku is attributed to Japan, the concept at the heart of the practice is not new. Many cultures have long recognized the importance of the natural world to human health.

Forest bathing isn't just for nature lovers; the practice can be as simple as walking in any natural environment and consciously connecting with what is around you.

Forest Bathing involves fully immersing oneself in nature, particularly in forests, to derive therapeutic benefits. Far from the idea of a simple walk in nature, Forest Bathing invites a deep sensory immersion. It's about slowing down, taking the time to observe, listen, smell and feel the nature around us.

During a Forest Bathing session, you walk slowly through the forest, paying particular attention to details and sensations. You can touch the trees, smell the scent of the vegetation, listen to the songs of the birds and simply immerse yourself in the calm and natural beauty. There is no specific goal or distance to cover, the objective is to connect with nature and let yourself be guided by its calming benefits.

The benefits of Forest Bathing are multiple. First of all, it helps reduce stress and anxiety by promoting a state of deep relaxation. Nature has a calming effect on our nervous system, decreasing levels of cortisol, the stress hormone.

Then, Forest Bathing strengthens our immune system by exposing us to an atmosphere rich in phytoncides, substances produced by trees which have beneficial effects on our health.

Additionally, this practice improves our focus, creativity, and mood, while promoting a sense of connection with the natural world.

To practice Forest Bathing, it is recommended to find preserved natural spaces, preferably forests rich in biodiversity. You can choose to do it alone, in a group or even with a specialized guide who will help you deepen your experience. Don't forget to put your cell phone and other technological distractions aside, so you can fully immerse yourself in the present moment and benefit as much as possible from the benefits of nature.

LOOKING AT SUNSETS AND SUNRISES

It can sometimes be difficult to notice your surroundings, no matter how beautiful they are. One of the most beautiful daily events to witness are sunrises and sunsets, but how many people stop to notice them?

Fortunately, this can change! If you want to take a little break from your hectic life to admire the natural beauty of a sunset, go for it! Your well-being will thank you.

Did you know that the vibrant colors of the changing sky during sunrises and sunsets and the serene ambiance during these times can evoke a deep sense of calm in you? A study found that watching sunsets in the evening and sunrises in the morning can improve your sense of "awe" about the universe, which can then lead to improvements in your health and well-being.

Watching a sunrise may not be possible if you're not an early riser. But admiring a sunset can be an easily achievable goal.

When you go outside, take a deep breath and watch the sunset, this can help your nervous system relax and allow you to handle your evening more calmly.

This is what meditation practice is for, and it allows you to reflect and be present. This can then help you appreciate the present moment and feel a sense of gratitude for the simple pleasures that life has to offer.

Watching sunrises and sunsets can be therapeutic, and by immersing yourself in the beauty of nature, you can experience a sense of calm, cultivate mindfulness, and promote gratitude. In a sometimes hectic and overwhelming world, who doesn't need moments of relaxation and quiet? Taking the time to witness the transition between day and night can be a powerful and beautiful tool for improving your mental health and emotional well-being.

So, the next time you get the chance, go outside and watch the magic of the sunrise or sunset and let yourself be captivated by the vibrant colors that paint the sky. Embrace beauty and let natural serenity brighten your day.

From reducing stress to improving sleep quality, here are some reasons why you should make watching the sunset part of your routine.

Watching the sunset can be a great way to reduce stress. Research suggests that exposure to nature, particularly natural light, can reduce stress and anxiety levels. Watching the sun slowly set behind the horizon can help you slow down, relax, and enjoy the beauty of nature, which can help reduce your stress levels.

Watching the sunset can also help improve your sleep quality. Sunsets produce a spectrum of red and orange light that can help regulate your circadian rhythm, also known as your body's internal clock. This can lead to more restful and restorative sleep.

Watching the sunset provides a great opportunity for reflection. The tranquility of the moment will allow you to avoid distractions and focus on your inner thoughts and feelings. It's a great way to reflect on your day, your accomplishments and your aspirations.

SINGING AND DANCING

Among other things, singing and dancing are two exercises that we can all practice at any time of the day or evening. We don't need to go out to do them. We can stay in our warm homes. We don't need to buy new clothes, or spend money on memberships that we know we won't honor. You can simply turn on the radio and off you go!

You may be wondering what the benefits of singing and dancing really are. For starters, we know that listening to music is an instant mood changer - putting on some Coldplay is probably less likely to make us jump into a room, laugh and smile, compared to, say, "Girls Just Wanna Have Fun " by Cyndi Lauper.

Music itself can promote a positive mental attitude. This has a fundamental effect on our brain, evoking memories and feelings that we would have otherwise forgotten.

The power of music is quite extensive and has been the subject of much research.

Studies have shown that music calms physical pain by releasing opioids (the body's natural painkiller), reducing stress and anxiety by lowering cortisol (stress hormone) levels, and increasing activity of memory.

This effect is extremely common in dementia patients, where music produces a positive effect on brain activity. In addition to listening to music, studies have shown that singing also improves short-term and working memory in dementia patients. Additionally, remember that reducing stress strengthens the immune system. It is always good to take!

A good, upbeat song will make you want to dance and sing like there's no one in the room with you. How do you feel? Pretty good, no doubt. Maybe even the thought of doing it now creates a little spark of positivity inside.

Endorphins are one of the four main hormones that promote pleasure, pain relief, and well-being (the others being serotonin, dopamine, and oxytocin). They are released into the body by the hypothalamus and pituitary gland, generally in response to physical activity.

Dancing to your favorite music will trigger the release of endorphins into the bloodstream, automatically improving your mood and bringing a positive mental attitude.

If you also sing the song, not only will you also release oxytocin (the bonding hormone), creating a feeling of confidence, but singing will also reduce cortisol levels, helping to reduce feelings of stress and anxiety. These two activities that we often take for granted as being a little frivolous are actually excellent supports for a calmer, happier and more positive mental attitude.

In addition to happy hormones, singing and dancing are excellent forms of self-expression. All these beautiful songs that have been written all come from someone's soul. It's a physical and mental way of expressing thoughts, feelings -

159

anything in fact - that might be bottled up inside. We all know that the best way to feel better is to express how we feel and for those of us who sometimes struggle to speak, it's almost certain that there will be a song that will make you the right words. Sometimes singing those lyrics or dancing to the music might be just what you need to do.

Dancing itself is a great full-body workout. It strengthens the leg and arm muscles and also develops core strength. The more we exercise, the stronger we become. Since dancing creates endorphins, we don't realize that we're giving our body the workout it needs to become fit and healthy, because we're having fun. Dancing is almost never a difficult exercise, unlike lifting weights or taking a HIIT class. This is often low impact, low stress but high cardio and agility.

So go ahead, put on those leggings and do a little jig – you'll feel a lot better for it!

As far as singing goes, it's actually good for the heart - not just emotionally (although that goes without saying). This helps keep your heart and lungs physically healthy. Singing promotes good posture and breathing technique.

Did you know that most of us have never learned to breathe properly? It sounds crazy, but it's something most of us have never learned. When you take a singing lesson - or even take a look on YouTube, the first thing a singer will teach you is how to stand and breathe properly. Breathing from your diaphragm means several things.

First, you get enough oxygen in your lungs so it can circulate throughout your body! Always useful.

Second, it relaxes our brain and emotions. The more oxygen we take in, the less efficiently we need to breathe. The less we breathe and the longer our inhale lasts, the calmer we feel. Just think about meditation for a moment. The relaxation technique always involves long, slow, deep breathing. We really should breathe like this all the time. Just imagine releasing stress all the time!

So, by breathing and standing properly, we reduce the strain on our body. Our circulation works better and lung capacity increases, as well as brain function. What a bonus!

So this is it. Just a few examples of the benefits that singing and dancing will bring you. You don't even need to spend hours doing it – although I guarantee that once you get started, you may not realize how long you've been doing it. Sometimes it's easy to get lost in the present moment!

There really are so many reasons that haven't even been covered here as to why singing and dancing is good for you. Here is a summary of some of them:

Music controls our mood – positive music makes us happy. It's a great instant cure for the blues.

It helps you express yourself. Any form of self-expression is so important for your well-being.

Exercise releases endorphins. Dancing to a song we love in a club or in our kitchen makes us feel good.

Songs can evoke memories and take us to places we had forgotten.

Research indicates that singing can strengthen the immune system, improving our overall health and happiness – which is ideal during the winter months.

Dancing is great for building energy – exercise increases energy levels and agility.

Dancing and singing are excellent for our memory.

Singing helps the respiratory system. It strengthens lung capacity, circulation and develops the ability to breathe properly, which allows more oxygen to enter our body.

Are you convinced? Come on, turn on the radio, find your favorite song, sing the lyrics and dance. You will feel 10 times better in just a few minutes. Guaranteed!

MANTRA SA TA NA MA

You don't need to be a yoga practitioner or deep into the chakras to enjoy the benefits of chanting a mantra!

Sa means Birth

Ta means Life

Na means Change or death in the sense "end of a stage"

Ma means rebirth

The obvious explanation is that each time we chant this mantra, we will complete a complete life cycle: from birth to rebirth. We find the idea of the inexorable succession of changes which form a cycle: birth, life, then death and finally rebirth.

The Sa Ta Na Ma mantra is used by those who want to accompany this natural change or for those who are undertaking a more profound change, whether spiritual or material. The mantra will help put the body, mind and energies in tune.

The art of chanting a mantra is called Japa Mantra.

It should be noted that this mantra has the particularity of blending perfectly with breathing. It might be an exaggeration to say that it is also a pranayama exercise, but when pronounced correctly, it can help hold one's breath during meditation. The simplicity of these four syllables is matched only by the power of the vibrations that pass through the body.

The first two syllables, SA TA must be said with the tongue in contact with the inside of the teeth.

The rhythm of this mantra is free. We can say it quickly to benefit from an overall vibration or to vibrate each syllable for a long time.

You should avoid practicing it before going to bed because it is an energizing mantra. For the rest, it can be associated with meditation or simply chanting with the help of a mala. Like other mantras, it can be said out loud or simply by chanting it internally.

This mantra is often associated with mudras, that is to say movements of the hands or fingers.

Its vibrational power allows you to work on your vagus nerve.

In addition to chanting the mantra, the practitioner will perform a specific mudra on each syllable that he will make last.

On the SA, you must perform the chin mudra, the thumb is against the index finger

On the TA, the middle finger will touch the thumb

On the NA, the ring finger comes into contact with the thumb

On the MA, the little finger is on the thumb

165

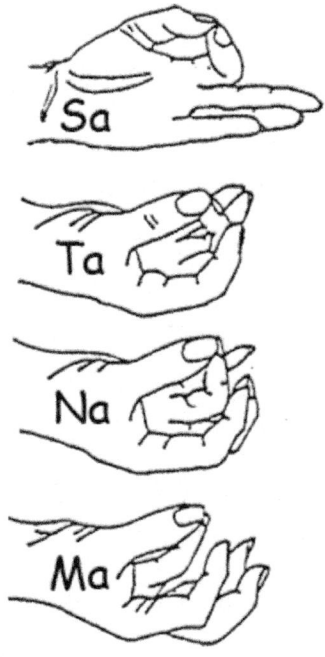

For the 12-minute Kirtan Kriya meditation:

Sit with your spine straight.

Start by saying 2 minutes out loud – SA TA NA MA

Then 2 minutes in an audible whisper – SA TA NA MA

4 minutes SILENT. Keep your hands and tongue moving – SA TA NA MA.

2 minutes Whisper – SA TA NA MA.

2 minutes out loud – SA TA NA MA.

Then for 30 seconds: Sit quietly. Stop making finger movements.

Over the next 30 seconds: inhale deeply, raise your arms in the air and shake your arms and fingers vigorously. You can involve the whole body and spine.

Exhale. Repeat 1 or 2 more times if desired. This is an important part of meditation because it helps move and release energy from the body.

You can of course do a shorter version of this meditation, 3 to 4 minutes is already very good!

Relax for a few minutes before starting your day. Or lie on your back.

CRYING

As a uniquely human phenomenon, crying is a natural response to a range of emotions, from deep sadness and grief to extreme happiness and joy.

But is crying good for your health?

The answer appears to be yes. The medical benefits of crying have long been known. Thinkers and doctors in ancient Greece and Rome claimed that tears act as a purgative, draining and purifying us. Current psychological thinking largely agrees, emphasizing the role of crying as a mechanism that allows us to release stress and emotional pain.

Crying is an important safety valve, largely because holding difficult feelings inside — what psychologists call repressive coping — can be bad for our health. Studies have linked repressive coping to a less resilient immune system, cardiovascular disease and hypertension, as well as mental health issues including stress, anxiety and depression.

Crying has also been shown to increase attachment behavior, encouraging closeness, empathy, and support from friends and family.

Scientists divide crying into three distinct categories: reflex tears, continuous tears, and emotional tears. The first two categories perform the important function of removing debris such as smoke and dust from our eyes and lubricating our eyes to protect them against infections. Their content is 98% water.

It's the third category, emotional tears (which flush stress hormones and other toxins from our system), that potentially offer the most health benefits. Researchers have established that crying releases oxytocin and endorphins. These feel-good chemicals help relieve physical and emotional pain.

As difficult as it can be, the best way to deal with difficult feelings, including sadness and grief, is to accept them. It's important to allow yourself to cry if you feel like it. Make sure you take time and find a safe space to cry if you need to.

Many people associate crying during grief with depression, when it can actually be a sign of healing.

Crying in the company of someone, or in the arms of a caring person, is even more beneficial. It is an act of vulnerability that makes us grow.

JOURNALING

Sometimes simple coping tactics can be helpful when you're stressed. Journaling is a habit that may be more useful than you think.

Journaling is an activity that many people have enjoyed for decades, whether it's organizing our thoughts or nurturing their writing skills.

Journaling simply means writing down your thoughts and feelings. This seemingly simple act has been shown to be beneficial for managing stress and coping with mental health issues.

Although journaling may seem like a chore at first, it has many benefits. Here's why journaling is good for you, plus tips for making it a habit.

Journaling can help you:

• identify fears or concerns that may be causing you stress or anxiety

• recognize triggers that exacerbate feelings of stress

• manage your stress more effectively in the future

• practice positive self-talk to boost your confidence

• identify and reduce unhelpful thoughts and behaviors

There are many types of journals that can help you relieve stress.

Although you can start with a simple notebook and pen, there are other types of journals that can help stimulate thinking and creativity. These include:

• bullet journals

• gratitude journals

• drawing journals

Once you've decided on a type of journal, you can consider establishing a routine. There are steps you can take to get into the habit of journaling to relieve stress, such as scheduling time to journal every day

Although it can sometimes be difficult to schedule time to journal, even spending a minute or two journaling each day can be beneficial.

Creating a schedule can help you maintain this habit, and keeping a journal can help you decompress and achieve mental clarity.

It can be a fun notebook, a real journal, a simple notepad or a spiral notebook – it doesn't matter what medium you write on.

You may also find it easier and more useful to journal on your smartphone, either through a designated journaling app or on your Notes app. But in general it is considered more beneficial to write by hand with a pen on paper.

Choose the format that suits you best and that you feel most comfortable with for writing your thoughts and feelings.

And remember, keeping a pen and paper – or your phone – handy is essential to developing and maintaining the habit of journaling.

Creating a routine for journaling is important.

But if it's too rigid, doesn't work well for you and ends up creating more stress, you have another option.

You can also journal whenever the mood strikes you.

A key element of journaling is consistency, but not necessarily structure. Keeping a regular journal can help you quickly identify themes.

Additionally, your journal doesn't need to follow a certain structure when it comes to how you write. Simply write down your words and ideas as they flow and come to you. Don't worry about spelling and grammar mistakes.

You can also use the space to draw if it helps improve your mood or stimulate creativity.

You can use your journal however you want. Although you don't have to share your journal with anyone, you may want to share some of your thoughts with your partner, close friends, or family members.

This can be especially helpful if you have difficulty talking about your feelings and prefer to write them down.

So, get started!

BINAURAL SOUNDS

Binaural sound therapy is an innovative approach in the field of sound therapy. It is based on the principle that each ear receives a slightly different sound frequency, but the brain merges them to create a unified perception of sound.

This mode of treatment is currently recommended to manage problems such as anxiety, stress and associated disorders. Typically, this self-help method is accessed via audio files listened to through stereo headphones.

The tones must be at frequencies below 1,000 hertz (Hz) for the brain to detect the binaural beat. The binaural beat perceived by a person corresponds to the difference in frequency between the waves entering the left ear and the right ear.

For example, if the left ear records sound at 200 Hz and the right ear at 210 Hz, the binaural beat is 10 Hz - the difference between the two frequencies.

Listening to binaural beats for a recommended period of time may affect a person's subsequent behavior and sleep cycles.

There are five different categories of frequency models:

Delta Pattern: Delta pattern binaural beats operate at a frequency of 0.5 to 4 Hz and are linked to dreamless sleep. In the study, people who received a delta-like frequency while sleeping entered a deeper phase of sleep, according to brain electroencephalogram (EEG) results.

Theta pattern: Practitioners tune binaural beats in the theta pattern at a frequency of 4 to 7 Hz. Theta rhythms help improve meditation, creativity, and sleep in the rapid eye movement (REM) phase.

Alpha Pattern: Alpha pattern binaural beats are tuned to a frequency of 7 to 13 Hz and can promote relaxation.

Beta Model: Beta Model binaural beats are at a frequency of 13 to 30 Hz. This frequency range can promote focus and alertness. However, it can also increase anxiety in higher frequencies.

Gamma pattern: This frequency pattern falls within a range of 30 to 50 Hz. These frequencies promote maintaining alertness when a person is awake.

The goal of binaural sound therapy may vary from person to person. Some people may need help reducing their anxiety, while others may want to increase their focus or deepen their level of meditation.

Proponents of binaural sound therapy suggest that the potential benefits include:

• reduction of stress and anxiety

• improved concentration and motivation

- improved self-confidence

- better long-term memory

- deeper meditation

- improvement in psychomotor performance and mood

To listen to binaural beats, a person needs a pair of stereo headphones and an MP3 player or other music system.

Here are some links if you want to give it a try

https://www.youtube.com/watch?v=4Gg4PEMJQag

https://www.youtube.com/watch?v=GYXTKnsAGWw

EFT OR TAPPING

Emotional Freedom Technique (EFT) is an alternative treatment for physical pain and emotional distress. We also talk about tapping or psychological acupressure.

People who use this technique believe that body tapping can create balance in your energy system and treat pain. According to its developer, Gary Craig, an energetic disturbance is the cause of all negative emotions and pain.

Although still under research, EFT tapping has been used to treat people suffering from anxiety and post-traumatic stress disorder.

Similar to acupuncture, EFT focuses on meridian points – or energetic hot spots – to restore your body's energy balance. It is believed that restoring this energetic balance can relieve symptoms that a negative experience or emotion may have caused.

According to Chinese medicine, meridian points are considered areas of the body where energy flows. These pathways help balance the flow of energy to maintain your health. Any imbalance can influence the disease.

Acupuncture uses needles to apply pressure to these energy points. EFT uses the fingertips to apply pressure.

Proponents say tapping helps you access your body's energy and send signals to the part of the brain that controls stress.

They claim that stimulating meridian points through EFT tapping can reduce stress or negative emotions you feel because of your problem, restoring balance to your disturbed energy.

EFT tapping can be divided into five stages. If you have more than one problem or fear, you can repeat this sequence to address it and reduce or eliminate the intensity of your negative feeling.

1. Identify the problem

For this technique to be effective, you must first identify the problem or fear you are experiencing. This will be your focal point while you tap. Focusing on one problem at a time is believed to improve your results.

2. Test the initial intensity

After identifying your problem, you need to set a baseline intensity level. The intensity level is rated on a scale of 0 to 10, with 10 being the worst or most difficult. The scale assesses the emotional or physical pain and discomfort you feel due to your main problem.

Establishing a baseline helps you track your progress after completing a full EFT sequence. If your initial intensity was 10 before tapping and ended at 5, you would have reached a 50% improvement level.

3. Preparation

Before you tap, you need to come up with a sentence that explains what you are trying to answer. It must focus on two main objectives:

• recognize problems

• accept yourself despite the problem

The common preparation phrase is: "Even though I have this [fear or problem], I accept myself deeply and completely. »

You can change this sentence to fit your problem, but it should not address anyone else's problem. For example, you cannot say, "Even though my mother is sick, I accept myself deeply and completely. » You need to focus on how the problem makes you feel in order to relieve the distress it causes.

It is best to approach this situation by saying, "Even though I am sad that my mother is sick, I accept myself deeply and completely.

4. EFT tapping sequence

The EFT tapping sequence involves methodically tapping the ends of nine meridian points.

There are 12 major meridians that reflect each side of the body and correspond to an internal organ. However, EFT primarily focuses on these nine:

- side of the hand, sometimes called "karate chop" (KC): small intestine meridian
- top of the head (TH): guiding vessel
- eyebrow (EB): bladder meridian
- side of the eye (SE): gallbladder meridian
- under the eye (EU): stomach meridian
- under the nose (UN): governing vessel
- chin (Ch): central vessel
- start of the clavicle (CB): kidney meridian
- under the arm (UA): spleen meridian

Start by tapping the side of your hand while simultaneously reciting your preparation phrase three times. Then, press each following point seven times, moving down the body in this ascending order:

- eyebrow
- side of the eye
- under the eyes
- under one's nose
- chin
- beginning of the clavicle
- under the arm

After tapping the armpit point, complete the sequence at the top of the head point.

While pressing the ascending points, recite a reminder phrase to stay focused on your problem. If your preparation sentence is: "Even though I am sad that my mother is sick, I deeply and completely accept myself," your reminder sentence might be: "The sadness I feel that my mother is sick."

Recite this phrase at each punch point. Repeat this sequence two or three times.

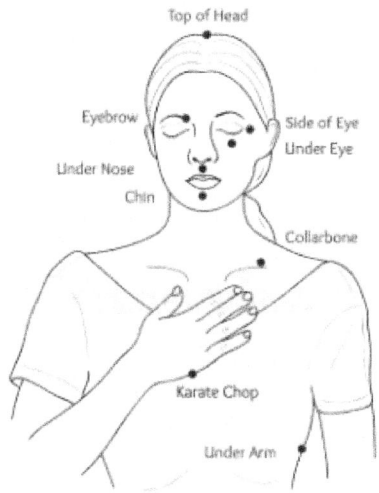

5. Test the final intensity

At the end of your sequence, rate your intensity level on a scale of 0 to 10. Compare your results with your initial intensity level. If you have not reached 0, repeat this process until you have reached it.

182

EFT is a separate technique, on which you could write an entire book, I advise you to look for a practitioner or a book on the subject if you are interested.

5 4 3 2 1 METHOD

The 54321 Method (or 5, 4, 3, 2, 1) is a basic exercise designed to manage acute stress and reduce anxiety. It involves identifying 5 things you can see, 4 things you can touch, 3 things you can hear, 2 things you can smell and 1 thing you can taste. In doing so, it helps you shift your attention from anxious thoughts to the present moment.

The 5 Senses Method is essentially another name for the 5, 4, 3, 2, 1 technique. It harnesses the power of your five senses (sight, touch, hearing, smell and taste) to divert your attention from distressing thoughts and emotions. By focusing on sensory experiences, the method aims to ground you in the here and now.

The 5, 4, 3, 2, 1 method works because it engages multiple senses, forcing you to focus on the current environment rather than dwelling on anxious thoughts. This interrupts the fight or flight response, calming the nervous system and reducing symptoms of anxiety or stress almost immediately. Additionally, it can be the first step toward long-term coping strategies for mental well-being.

This five-step exercise can be very helpful during times of anxiety or panic by helping you ground yourself in the present when your mind bounces between various anxious thoughts.

Before you begin this exercise, pay attention to your breathing. Slow, deep, long breaths can help you maintain a sense of calm or return to a calmer state. Once you've regained your breath, follow these steps to help ground you:

Recognize FIVE things you see around you. It could be a pen, a dot on the ceiling, anything in your environment.

Recognize FOUR things you can touch around you. It could be your hair, a pillow, or the ground beneath your feet.

Recognize THREE things you hear. It could be any external sound. If you hear your stomach rumbling, it counts! Focus on things you can hear outside of your body.

Recognize TWO things you can smell. Maybe you're in your office and you smell a pencil, or maybe you're in your bedroom and you smell a pillow. If you need to take a brief walk to find a scent, you might smell soap in your bathroom or nature outside.

Recognize ONE thing you can taste. What does your mouth taste like: gum, coffee, or a lunch sandwich?

This letting go technique is relatively effective in calming immediate anxiety. Diverting our attention from useless and often arbitrary thoughts to focus on something concrete demonstrates the sterility of ruminating thoughts.

HOW TO INCORPORATE ALL THIS IN YOUR DAILY LIFE

You now have a whole range of tools at your disposal to soothe your body and mind.

You just have to incorporate them into your life and it may seem a little complicated at first.

The big advantage of all these techniques is that they are free, accessible to all, and that they do not require any particular equipment, any specific outfit, etc...

If you want to create a routine that is easy to follow and doesn't take up too much time during the day, here is an example of what you can do.

We can start our day with a few minutes of breathing/meditation upon waking up, we choose a technique that allows us to start off on the right foot, anchored in our parasympathetic nervous system.

Then we get up, we can walk barefoot, already in our house, possibly a few steps outside if we have a garden and the weather permits, bonus if we can also see the sunrise!

While breakfast is heating, you can take the opportunity to do a little shaking, to wake up the body or some Gi Gong Swing or Tai Chi Twist.

A little cold water on the face and/or body at the end of the shower and you are ready for a busy day full of serenity!

At mid-day, it can be interesting to take a quick look at yourself, to calm the nervous system again.

You can take your break outside, take a few steps in nature if you can.

5 minutes of cardiac coherence or Darth Vader breathing with some soothing music or binaural sounds in the ears. Again a little shaking or seated pendulum or a few minutes of whirling dervish.

The day is over, it's time to relax.

A little tree pose while dinner is being prepared or a goddess pose while waiting for everyone to be at the table!

Before going to bed, a few hip-opening postures, such as the eye of the needle, which can be combined with a few minutes of deep diaphragmatic breathing, 2 in 1 effect!

We can end with a few minutes of rocking the happy baby with his legs on the wall.

If you have encountered anger during your day, you can also release the pressure by making tiger growls or lion breathing.

All that remains is to lay your head on the pillow for a good night's rest!

Obviously this is just an example, and some exercises will speak to you more than others.

I like to multitask when I do my exercises, meaning most of the time for exemple, I do coherent breathing while I do the rocking on all 4 and the whirling dervish, and I meditate while sitting in the grass outside, so I ground at the same time!

Some will be more suitable depending on how your day went. Sometimes you will need to energize yourself and other times you will need to relax more.

It's up to you to dig into this book to find the exercises your body needs every day, that's the whole objective of this toolbox!

Create your routine, play with it and enjoy the benefits of a calm and balanced nervous system.

SPECIAL SHITTY DAY ROUTINE

<u>My prescription:</u>

- Pillow slams or Shadow Boxing to get rid of anger

- Tiger Growl x 3

- Darth Vader breathing 5 minutes

- Add a few minutes of legs at the wall before bed

ROUTINE WHEN YOU ARE NOT MOTIVATED

<u>My prescription:</u>

- Whirling Dervish 3 minutes

- Standing Shaking for 2 minutes or Qi Gong Swing (

- Clap and rub your hands for 2 minutes

- Splash your face with cold water

Go, you rock!

ROUTINE WHEN YOU FEEL SAD

My prescription:

• Bamboo in the wind and hug for 2 minutes

• Rocking Cobra for 2 minutes

• Rocking on all fours 3 minutes

• Cry, if necessary, while massaging and caressing your body (p.82)

ROUTINE WHEN YOU GET SCATTERED

My prescription:

• Tree in the wind 1 minute on each side

• Hip circles 2 minutes

• Fire Goddess 2 minutes

• Resonant Breathing or SA TA NA MA 3 minutes

And presto, focus!

ROUTINE STRESS AT WORK, ANXIETY ++

My prescription:

• Half Salamander

• Double inhale and sigh

• A little shaking and shrugging shoulders hidden in the toilets or in the open space ;-)

• A little binaural sounds in the ears and the 5 4 3 2 1 or EFT method if you feel yourself having a panic attack.

Relax!

SPECIAL ROUTINE LONG SITTING STATION, LONG ROUTE ETC...

My prescription:

• Leg swings in music

• Rocking on all 4 if possible

• Tai Chi twist

• Butterfly Bridge and Thread the Needle

+ a nice bath as a bonus!

191

INSOMNIA ROUTINE

My prescription:

• Seated Forward Fold 2 minutes

• Rocking Happy baby and reclining twist 5 minutes

• Legs at the wall with diaphragmatic breathing 5 minutes or Meditation of your choice

• Breathing 4 7 8 or Voo Sound

And ZZzzzzzzzzzz

MANTRAS TO REPEAT TO YOURSELF WHEN YOU FEEL STRESSED

I'm calm

I am safe

I am enough

I have valuable

I have the necessary resources within me

I am full of life

I am peaceful

I am loved

Thank you for the alert, dear nervous system, but I got this!

BREATHE

WALK OUTSIDE

SIGH

SHAKE YOURSELF

MOVE

WRITE

STRETCH

YAWN

HYDRATE YOURSELF

AAAAAAHHHHHHH

EXPRESS YOUR NEEDS

GROWL

CRY

ACCEPT

LOVE

MAKE SPACE

Printed in Great Britain
by Amazon

45670654R00109